BREAKING THE
NO BARRIER

BREAKING THE
NO BARRIER

Walter Hailey

Triamid Press

Chicago • Dallas

BREAKING THE NO BARRIER
The Billion Dollar Battle Plan For Getting Everyone You Want To Say YES To Your Proposition

Copyright (©) 1992
Third Edition 1994

Book design by Kelly Rickert
Cover design by Sam Concialdi

Published by Triamid Press, Chicago - Dallas

ISBN: 1-882306-00-7

Library of Congress Catalog Card Number: 92-61988

Printed in the United States of America

ACKNOWLEDGEMENTS

Those closest to me started contributing to this book long before I conceived of writing it. Their contributions began back on the cotton farm in Mesquite, Texas, where I was born. Without friends and family who taught me, gave spiritual guidance and discipline, I would never have known enough success to justify writing a book. This book owes a great deal to the teachings and writings of great business and motivational thinkers, past and present, too many to name. David Keener, my lifelong business partner and mentor, deserves special thanks. My ideas would have come to less without his awesome practicality and capacity for hard work. My associate Steve Anderson convinced me that a book about my NEER system was an idea whose time has come — and he kept pushing until the idea was reality. A special thanks goes to recent new mentors Dr. Mac Lee and Dr. Peter Dawson, who have been instrumental in helping us develop niche markets for our products and services. Thanks to Mike Steere for his help in translating spoken Texas into written English. Above all, thanks are owed to my beloved wife, Barbara, upon whose encouragement and support all of my successes are founded.

BREAKING THE NO BARRIER

By Walter B. Hailey

Part Two: From Fear To NEER

To all my mentors, too numerous to mention here.

INTRODUCTION

Be Your Own Marketing Director

Don't Read This Book

If your boss is doing his or her job, you can quit reading right here.

If management is doing what it ought to be doing — working to create markets for the company's products as hard as you're working to sell those products, so you've got access to all the qualified, nonresistant clients you need — put this book back on the shelf.

Move over to where they keep the books on investing. Your problem (if you've got a problem) is what to do with all the money you're making.

Enjoy.

LIFE AND INNER DEATH OF A SALESMAN

Still with us? So are 97 percent of salespeople, and anyone else who needs to hear "Yes" to make a living, who are becoming the financial and psychological casualties of one of the cruelest crises in the history of American business. An entire generation of Persuaders (my own word for salespeople and those in allied fields) is being sacrificed by companies that do nothing to foster their employees' success — or even survival! — in current hypercompetitive markets. Most companies don't help their people on the job. They don't train their people so they can help themselves.

A couple of pages back I dedicated this book to my mentors, the men and women who bumped me along the way from a cotton farm east of Dallas to a wonderful bounty of personal and business rewards. My business life, which always involved selling, led to ownership of a company that sold for $78 million. (I didn't want to let it go just then, but everybody has a choking point. Mine happens to be $78 million.) Without those mentors, I would never have gotten where I am. I have listed those to whom I owe most at the back of this book.

That's who the book is **to**.

Who it's **for**, is my friend Charlie.

The name Charlie isn't real, but the man is. And so is his story:

It started last year, when Planned Marketing Associates, my professional development corporation, was about to do a one-day seminar on career strategies in a large Southwestern city. We decided to offer an advance promotional evening program, free of charge, with the sponsorship of a hotel and radio station. The 300 hundred folks who turned out for the preview ran the gamut, from kids just out of high school to executive-suite types in shaky businesses, who knew that a job change might be in their immediate future.

A few minutes after the program started, a tall, good-looking fellow walked in and sat down. That fellow was Charlie. If a marketing director wanted to build his own ideal sales representative from scratch, he'd come up with somebody just like this. Charlie was appealingly young, but also reassuringly mature, thanks to some premature gray. His Brooks Brothers–type suit, which was plenty sharp to begin with, looked better because it was hanging on him.

Charlie got to talking with Steve Anderson, a key man here at Planned Marketing Associates, and Steve introduced him to me. Better than the looks and clothes, to my way of thinking, was the invisible number that Charlie wore on his forehead. This is what I always look for when I meet people, the life score they give themselves. Charlie, that first night, was wearing a big, bright nine. Nine, which says "great," but not "perfect," is my favorite number, for everyday use. (Ten, if you try to keep it up there all the time, can be quite a load.) I trusted Charlie, I liked him, and I saw in him tremendous potential as a Persuader.

Charlie told us about his current situation and his aspirations. He was a top producer for his company, selling class rings and caps and gowns to schools all over the region. In his field he was almost phenomenally successful — the living he made, by anybody's standards, was comfortable. But Charlie wanted more. He wanted to raise his career stakes, both in challenge and financial rewards, but he'd already reached the top of the Graduation Day business. So Charlie was looking to make a change. He was looking at insurance, where the rewards for sales success can be fantastically high.

Insurance sales happens to be where I scored my ultimate business successes.

Charlie and our Planned Marketing team kept in touch while he thought through and made his move. He studied and earned his license, and got offers from the better agencies in his city.

Eventually he decided to represent one of the most respected national insurance companies. Given his potential, and the quality of the company, Charlie's move could have been very good for everybody involved.

Thirty days of silence. Then we got a call from someone who used Charlie's name, but otherwise bore only a distant resemblance to the man we'd been talking to. Could he see us, as soon as possible? We were, in fact, going back to Charlie's city, but on a very tight schedule. If Charlie hadn't sounded so miserable, to the point of desperation, we would have told him there wasn't time for a meeting.

He looked even worse than he sounded. He forced a smile, while everything but his mouth was saying how much he hated life, and maybe himself, just then. He was actually stooped over, like an old man! His forehead number was too low to read. Charlie clearly needed to talk, but was too down to tell his story on his own. We had to keep asking him questions.

Things began pretty encouragingly at the insurance company, which gave Charlie a thorough product schooling and "tools," before he went out to sell. He learned everything he'd ever need to know about the company's financial instruments — policies, investment programs, etc. He got all sorts of flip charts and brochures. His gorgeous presentation kit came in an even more gorgeous genuine leather case. With his head full of numbers and technical information, and an armload of cowhide and printed-matter, Charlie went forth.

Like every other neophyte selling financial services, he started making presentations to his family and friends. He went at it with a will — laziness will never be this man's downfall.

When we saw him, Charlie had made **one hundred** presentations.

But he hadn't made **one** sale!

He was going broke. Much worse than that, though, was the

inner damage. Every "No" he heard was a stab to his self-esteem. By the time we saw him, he had a hundred stab wounds, none of them healing. Poor Charlie's ego had been bled to the point that "No" was the only answer anybody could give him, because "No" was what he was asking for, in attitude and body-language. He had friends who refused to grant the courtesy of listening to him talk about insurance for five minutes!

Charlie was, in a word, a wreck, and making himself a worse wreck by blaming himself. The company, after all, had given him what he needed — hadn't it? So the failure had to be Charlie's own fault.

Didn't it?

Millions Of Charlies

I was, naturally, sad about what had happened to Charlie. I felt some responsibility, too, because my own successes in insurance probably encouraged him to make a career change. But more than feeling sad, or responsible, I was angry. No, angry isn't a strong enough word. I was irate. Incensed. Furious.

There was, indeed, somebody to blame for what had happened. But it sure wasn't Charlie.

I knew exactly where the blame belonged because I once walked in Charlie's shoes. Before I developed my own marketing system — which is the subject of this book — the insurance business nearly destroyed me, the way it was destroying him. And I knew who to blame because I once owned my own insurance company, and had other people selling for me. I knew, too, because I've spent the last five years training other people's employees to sell, patching up the holes put in salespeople by the folks they work for.

The fault, in Charlie's tale of woe, lies with his company. It lies, more specifically, with the home-office middle manager types who taught him everything **but** what he needed to know.

For all the hours of numbers and how to use the flip charts, he didn't get five minutes of training in one-on-one communication, which is the essence of selling. He heard what he ought to **tell** prospects without hearing a thing about how he ought to **ask** about people's total insurance needs, so he could begin showing them solutions to their total insurance problems. If two-way-communication is the essence, problem-solving is the soul of sales-manship, and all persuasion in business. With neither working for him, Charlie's chances of hearing "I'll take it" were slim.

His chances went down to slim-to-none because he didn't have a clue about who he should make presentations to. Just as bad, he didn't know anything about how to make sure his presentations were welcomed, and heard with complete attention and **respect.** It's likely that Charlie's own God-given talents would have brought him some success, if he'd knocked on a few of the right doors, with the right sort of preparation, which would have enhanced his pres-tige in the eyes of the customers. But he talked to whoever would listen. Even though he knew his prospects, all his calls turned stone cold. Charlie's presentations were dead on arrival.

The home office had, in effect, thrown their new agent into a wide and deadly dangerous ocean. They told him he had life-saving gear — but the stuff they gave him didn't float! It would have been more honest, and kinder, to skip the preliminaries and the leather presentation case and tell Charlie and the other new hires to sink or swim. That way they might have gone somewhere for swimming lessons. As it was, Charlie went into the water thinking he had what he needed to survive. We caught him going down for the third time.

This unnecessary suffering makes me angry. What makes me madder still is that those who set up Charlie to take his fall will never share the suffering. They're guilty as sin, but they're safe, both financially and psychologically. The company will stand by them, even though they don't do business a bit of good. In the short run it's easy and comfortable to keep middle management fat and happy. In the long run, it's big trouble.

One story like Charlie's is a personal tragedy. A few million is a national tragedy. And millions of Charlies is what we've got, in every industry that involves direct selling.

Things are as bad as they are in insurance in every other industry that relies on salespeople to create their own markets. Newcomers are lured by high commissions and smooth-talking recruiters. But then success, when you don't know how to work toward it, is just a mirage.

The cost in dollars of inadequately prepared new sales forces is enormous. Fortune 500 companies waste well over $150 million annually on first-year dropouts, who fail largely because of lack of training and supervision. It has been estimated that $50,000 is spent annually on each new employee, half of whom won't make it through the year. Beyond the early washouts are under-performing veteran sellers. Every sales call costs about $250, but 6 in 10 calls conclude without the seller asking for an order or commitment. It has been known for decades that 20 percent of our employees do 80 percent of the money-making business. Much more shocking is the estimate that 5 percent bring home 50 percent of the business! These statistics couldn't be worse if we were working at making them worse.

Of course the biggest price is not paid in dollars — but in stress, disappointment and heartbreak. What companies **don't** do to prepare their salespeople takes a terrible toll on the lives of both sellers and their loved-ones. A good deal of what's wrong with salespeople, away from work, is directly traceable to what's wrong at work.

Ask your neighbors. Look to your left and to your right, and you'll see someone who has failed in sales.

I made my fortune selling insurance. But, looking back, I

wouldn't go through the pain and strain of starting over, without adequate training or marketing support from my management. I at least had a shot, back in the Fifties and Sixties. The climate back then was a good deal more forgiving. Business weather these days is awful, for under-prepared persuaders. If you want to survive you'd better put yourself through Survival School. But the companies go on giving new sellers exactly what they gave me.

If I were a neophyte today, I would not even consider going to work for a company that wasn't going to provide me with a **qualified market.** I would rather run a service station at night in Frostbite Falls, Minnesota, in February, than go out and be rejected over and over again because my boss won't do a thing to help me find qualified clients. Like any good Texan, I don't like the cold. But I hate cold-calling rejection worse.

Be Your Own Head Office

A while back I told you who this book is **to.** My mentors. I never would have made it without them. You won't make it without mentors of your own.

It's **for** my friend Charlie. I hope it will do him and his peers some good, both emotionally and financially.

Now I'll tell you who the book is **against.**

It's against **RAMs.**

RAM is our acronym for **Re-Active Manager.** RAMs are the bad guys in this and most other stories about what's wrong in American business. A RAM — no, a bunch of RAMs (they don't like to do things on their own) — put the hurt on poor Charlie.

RAM, of course, isn't only an acronym. RAMs are he-sheep, those critters with big curly horns for making a show and banging on other rams. If you're in the herd, this is one powerful, impressive authority figure. If you're not, he's pretty much a sheep, mutton and wool and dumb as a bag of rocks. He'll go wherever a sheepdog chases him.

Substitute the horns for Brooks Brothers suits and $250 shoes.

Think of the head-butting and showing-off as office politics and conference room speeches.

Remind you of anyone you know?

What a RAM won't do is go out and **make** something happen, on his or her own (offices have she-RAMs, too).

Absolutely nothing is going to happen, if you don't go out and find an opportunity and make it happen. If you don't, somebody else will. The easy sales are gone. The easy deals have been done. RAMs, somehow or another, never got the message.

We could make fun of RAMs for the next 200 pages, and maybe another book or two after this one. But we'll leave that to someone else.

We're going to do, right now, what you have to do if there's a RAM in your life.

Forget about him or her.

Don't let somebody else's failures get in the way of your success.

If you wait for the boss to provide you with training and prospects, you're never going to be better than mediocre.

You've got to do what needs doing yourself. You've got to be your own marketing director. This is what this book will teach you to be.

I have seen many top sellers who weren't great salesmen, but who had great markets and who were very successful. But I have never seen a great salesman who did great with poor markets.

A top salesperson without good, creative market development behind him or her is like a .300 hitter on a bad team. His average is terrific, sure, but he doesn't get up to bat often enough. In baseball terms, selling is what happens when you get to the plate. Marketing is how often you get to the plate. You must have both.

NEER™

NEER is an acronym for my **Naturally Existing Economic Relationship** marketing system. It will get you from wherever you are now to as many contacts you need with low-resistance, qualified buyers. NEER, the way I used it in my businesses, and the way we teach it in Planned Marketing's seminars, eliminates cold calling, and all the wasted time and emotional injury that goes with it.

NEER made me a multimillionaire, from scratch, but I didn't develop it to get rich. I started developing NEER because of a terrible case of cold-call hypothermia. One night one too many strangers told me "No!" and it hit me like the whole world saying "No!" to everything about Walter Hailey. It was, in fact, an East Texas pig farmer, who didn't want a Lone Star Life insurance policy.

This guy never even invited me into his house. I made my presentation in the car, and put seven textbook closes on him. If he'd been to sales training, the way I had, he might have known I was closing, and that he was supposed to say, "I'll take it." But all I got was "No!" with all sorts of silent messages that pig farmers were kings and princes compared to insurance salesmen, who were right down there with the hogs and pigs.

Maybe he had had a bad day. Maybe, for that matter, he was being as friendly as he knew how, and I only imagined he was being ornery. Whatever the problem was, it didn't have to be mine — except I made it mine, and took it down the road with me, feeling awful.

But then lightning struck. Driving down Highway 67 from Rockwall in the dark, I swore never to let this happen to me again. No human was going to make me think less of me.

Nobody.

Ever.

By that time I wasn't a kid anymore. I'd been selling most of my life, with some successes. But the night with the pig farmer started my real, grown-up sales career. First I began to study my field, reading Napoleon Hill's **THINK AND GROW RICH** and other writings of great business-wise men. Hill inspired me to form a Master Mind group, where friends and I shared advice and emotional support for our businesses and life in general. Instead of throwing myself at work, headlong, I started thinking about what I was doing, organizing my efforts, and working toward definite goals.

My most successful NEER was a system for selling insurance to retail grocers through their wholesale food distributors. The deal was "Win-Win-Win." Everybody — our insurance company, the wholesalers, the grocers — made money, saved money, or both. NEER didn't come to me overnight, and it didn't work the first couple times I tried it, because I tried it in the wrong places, with the wrong people. I didn't give up, though. And when my NEER was up and running, our closing ratio went to 8 in 10. (If you sell, you know that these are numbers to die for.) NEER worked because I was working within a system where people were already doing business with each other, and knew and liked and trusted each other.

NEER™ Is Human Leverage

The first person who ever told me about NEER was my daddy, when I was a boy. I had no idea he was teaching me a marketing system. He didn't, either.

He said, "Son, the intelligent know *everything*. The wise and the rich know *everybody*, and know them favorably and with respect."

NEER is a way of meeting the right people, the right way, in order to know them the right way. With NEER, selling isn't selling so much as knowing people better. Knowing them, and helping them solve their business problems, while you're solving your own. NEER brings a confidence in person-to-person contacts that you've probably never known. You can be sure of yourself and your product, service and ideas. You can be sure that you'll be welcomed, and heard with good will and respect. NEER contacts are always worthwhile, for both seller and prospect.

I like to think of NEER as a new definition for "leverage." Once upon a time this was a great word. Archimedes said, "Give me a lever long enough and I'll move the world!" But then the 1980s gave leverage a bad name. Leverage meant debt. It also meant a lot of people losing their jobs and some rich guys going to jail. Now maybe we can rehabilitate the word, which is, when you think about it, a pretty good word.

Leverage is about multiplying forces, so you can do things that would break your back if you tried to do them without leverage.

NEER is **human leverage**, applied to business relationships.

NEER™ Is Where You Need To Be

We will get you from wherever you are to — and **through** — your most important doors. The persuasive business you do, once you're through those doors, is up to you. I can guarantee that you'll do more of your business, whatever it is, because you're getting through more of the right kind of doors, and the people who open them are glad to see you.

Because NEER is more than a selling system, this is not, strictly speaking, a selling book. Lord knows enough of them have been written. Buy all you want. Some of them are very informative. But the trouble with most selling systems — and sales training in general — is that the programs start with the seller comfortably in front of the buyer, who is all ears.

Most sales training subscribes to the mistaken notion that selling is what happens when you get in front of somebody.

Wrong.

Selling is preparation. Most of the quality time and planning effort should be spent **before** the presentation. Remember Charlie? He probably had all the presentations and closings he needed. The critical information, which he didn't have, is how to get close enough to the right kind of prospects, in mutual harmony and communication, with prestige and rapport. NEER will get you there.

This book, like NEER, is about meeting the right people, the right way, in the right circumstances.

The first person to meet is yourself. Part One, **Programming Your Two-Billion-Dollar Computer,** shows how to learn more about what you ought to be doing from what you're already doing. Most of us don't know what we know, and how valuable that knowledge is. Experience might be the greatest teacher, but we're the worst students. And the tuition is very high. Part One also teaches new ways to observe and process what's going on, so we can learn from experience **while** it's happening. What we're offering, basically, is a new set of software, to get you operating in real time. God gave us a wonderful piece of hardware. No man-made computer comes close, in power and speed, to what you've got between your ears. But the brain isn't any better than its programming, and what you put into it. The goal of Part One is to develop an active and inquiring and **trained** mind.

Part Two, **From Fear To NEER**, introduces and explains my NEER Marketing System, which was responsible for my own success in selling. Since I decided to reveal this system, I have seen it bring startling results to those who sell virtually every product and service. NEER has also worked wonders for thousands of other professionals, from teachers to doctors to police officers. Since the NEER system applies to any sort of business that relies on persuasion (tough to think of a business that doesn't, isn't it?) this book uses the word **Persuader** about as often as **Seller**. The words are almost interchangeable because the ways to **persuade** another person to say "Yes!" are just about universal, whether or not selling is involved.

We're so confident of NEER's power that we guarantee our clients at least a 20 percent increase in sales, or however they measure career accomplishment.

NEER has a dual benefit to sellers and other professionals.

• First, it takes the anguish out of making new business contacts. For sellers this means no more anxiety-ridden cold calling, and no more call reluctance, which has stalled many careers in sales.

• Second, NEER makes each business contact more rewarding, by vastly increasing the percentage of contacts who say "Yes" to your product, service or idea. Each "Yes" will bring you more business than before, because NEER puts you in touch with your dream clientele, the influential and wealthy individuals who can do your business — whatever it is — the most good.

With NEER, what was once emotionally taxing work becomes genuinely **fun**. Not only is it fun, it is vastly more productive and financially rewarding. You'll do more, and earn more, with less emotional wear-and-tear.

The NEER system expands from prospecting for valuable business contacts to prospecting for **ideas.** Finding the Mother Lode of business- and life-enhancing ideas is a simple matter of **asking**. The answers to many of our most perplexing business and personal questions are as close as our professional peers and friends. My business was stalled until Napoleon Hill's *Think And Grow Rich* inspired me to join with other local business people in a Master Mind group, where we shared ideas and enthusiasm. Without the support of that group, my career might never have taken off. Besides showing the immense creative power of groups of like-minded individuals, the final pages of this book explain the critical importance of one-on-one relationships with mentors. Somewhere there's an expert in whatever you need to know, who is, most likely, anxious to share that knowledge with you. Mentors illustrate one of NEER's central philosophical tenets:

What you seek is seeking you. What you're looking for, is looking for you.

Mess Up This Book

Not too long ago I told you not to buy this book — unless, of course, you **need** it.

Now that I know you need it, I want you to make a mess out of it.

I can't ask you to stand up and holler, the way we do every hour or so at the seminars, to drive points home and get the blood circulating. But I am asking you to get involved with what you read, and to show your involvement with notes, underlinings, fluorescent highlighting, circles, pictures. Write down "Yes!" when you're really with me, and "No!" when you're against me, and whatever else comes to mind. This is **your** book, and it ought to be personalized cover-to-cover, to the point that nobody else would want to read it. Each chapter has interactive exercises, with space for written answers, but the whole book is meant to be written on. "You" are my co-author. Your job is to write the part of the book which I can't write for you — how this material applies to your own situation, and what specific good it can do for you.

I suggest getting yourself a green pen and a red pen, and writing down what you want to **start** doing in green, what you want to **stop** in red. The two-color system works pretty well. Feel free to expand on it. I'd like to think that somewhere out there my book is lit up with color, like the rainbow.

Of course the most important marks you make won't be in the book, but in the world. The point of every chapter, subchapter and exercise — indeed, the point of every word — is to make you more effective on the job, whatever your job is. This is, in the truest sense of the word, a **work**book. It's meant to make you work smarter and better and, above all, happier.

This book is meant to be educational, in the word's best sense. The true purpose of education is **action**. Knowledge, if you don't put it to good use, is an empty thing. I am asking you to take **action** with what your learn from these pages. Don't just do it once — do it over and over, until it's an ingrained habit. And don't wait to start using our NEER techniques. Do it now! As soon as you read something new, get it off the page and into your life.

PART ONE

PROGRAMMING YOUR TWO - BILLION - DOLLAR COMPUTER

1

The Owners Manual You Never Got

THE MOST MAGNIFICENT MACHINE

Not too many years ago, when I was still officially numbered among the young, I was an active member of the Young President's Organization. I attended a YPO meeting in London, where somebody asked the executive in charge of IBM in Europe what it would take to build a computer with the storage capacity of the human brain.

Such a machine, the IBM executive said, might cost $2 billion. It would be more or less the size of the Empire State Building in New York. It would generate so much heat that you'd have to divert the Hudson River to cool it. The IBM man was really telling us that a computer as smart as we are wasn't yet feasible. There have since been giant advances in thinking machines. But the one that matches the awesome human brain is still a fantasy. Even if such a super-computer is eventually built, nobody this side of the Pentagon will be able to afford one.

The bottom line here is never going to change:

You can't afford to buy what God **gave** you. You own the most magnificent thinking machine in the universe.

Time on an artificial brain, if they ever do build one, will be a good deal more than a $1 a second. This means you get, for free, at least a million dollars worth of thinking every 12 days, a billion dollars every 32 years.

We Are All Born Rich!

But most of us don't convert our capital to money, or anything else worthwhile.

The biggest problem, with your free $2 billion computer, is that you don't get an owners manual.

We have to learn how to run our brains, how to program them and take in information and retrieve it and **use** it. With disciplined mental techniques, the brain is by far the most powerful tool in the universe. With none, it's about as good as that home computer gathering dust because you never figured out what it was good for.

No, an unused brain is a lot worse. When you shut off a Tandy 1000, it's off. But a brain is never off.

Idle hands, they say, are the devil's playground. An idle brain is more like the devil's Walt Disney World.

The brain is always sending you messages, 2,000 words a minute. Unregulated, the talk is almost all bad — one estimate says that 84 percent of our internal vocalizations are negative. Besides talking us down, an untrained brain likes to listen to other folks down-talking. It will tune out valuable input, replay past failures, follow bad habits and load us down with all sorts of irrelevant worries, fears and feelings of low self-worth. The most valuable tool, if you don't learn how to use it, is also the biggest obstacle to happiness and success.

It has always struck me as odd that colleges and universities teach us so little about thinking, plain old thinking. The emphasis is brain-stuffing, not brain-using. Sure, there are courses in Logic, but that's really more about working out abstractions on paper than decision-making in real life. Nobody is teaching people to think! I'm talking about real-world thinking, that's useful in the real world, right now.

A little wrong-headedness, in some jobs, won't do you too much harm. In sales, it's very serious, because selling **is** thinking, fast and creatively and on your feet. You don't need a college degree but you need an education. You need what we call **CPA**. **C**reative **P**rospecting **A**ctivity.

The first step to success with the NEER system (or success with anything else, for that matter) is to put your own mental house in order, so your mind can do you a maximal amount of good.

• Garbage in, garbage out. What they say about computers is true, in spades, about your mind.

But you can take it a few steps farther:

• Nothing in, garbage out. If you don't give it **good** data, the brain makes up its own bad stuff.

• Garbage already **in**. This is important to remember. If you've lived to voting age, you've got a lifetime worth of mental and emotional refuse.

I don't know who gave us all these slogans that keep echoing in our heads. If I knew, I'd give them all back! "What you don't know won't hurt you." Reflect a moment on that one. Could anything be **less** true? What you don't know can kill you. "Ignorance is bliss," is a variation on the same theme. Here's a real gem: "Children should be seen and not heard." This is a recipe for raising idiots. I could go on and on. Subconscious slogan thinking has our minds so filled with bad stuff that it's hard for us to get in anything good.

The other kind of stuff that needs to be thrown out are the old grievances, angers and feelings of shame that get between you and your aspirations. One of the first things we do at our three-day Power of Persuasion seminars is to ask participants to "Chunk Your Junk." They write down their worst piece of "junk" and throw it in big galvanized metal garbage can, at the front of the seminar room. The can looks like it's holding a few scraps of paper and a lot of air, but, in the psychological dimension, it weighs a million tons. It would overflow three landfills.

A little junk-chunking wouldn't be a bad start for you readers. You'll notice that the next page is blank, on both sides.

Write down your meanest, most burdensome piece of trouble —unresolved anger, grudge, guilt, whatever.

Now rip the page out. Crumple it up and do what you should have done a long time ago. Throw it out.

I think I'm feeling a little hanging-back. Maybe, even though nobody else is in the room, this sort of thing embarrasses you. Or maybe you think that junk-chunking, the way we do it, is just plain silly. Believe me, though, there's nothing to be embarrassed about, and the exercise is anything but silly. Symbolic acts like this can be enormously important. The subconscious mind pays attention, and does what you are acting out.

So what have you got to lose?

Chunk your junk.

Of course sometimes junk is like that old alley cat you feel sorry for and feed. It keeps coming back. If it does, chunk it until it stays chunked.

JUNK
Write it down...

_____

_____

_____

_____

_____

_____

_____

_____

_____

_____

_____

_____

...now chunk it!

The Five-Minute Ophthalmologist

Read the following sentence out loud, fast:

Finished files are the result of years of scientific study combined with the expertise of many years of experts.

Count the Fs. How many did you get?

2, 3, 4, 5, 6 or 7?

In our seminars we get all six answers, every time we try the exercise. About 10 percent see only two Fs! I was among these 10 percenters when Lou Tice, the well-known human relationship expert, first showed me the exercise. My wife Barbara beat me by one F. She found 3.

Grownups shouldn't have too much trouble counting letters, but they do. The first time they read the sentence, most people miss the Fs in "of." Their eyes are looking right at the letters, but their ears are hearing the "v" sound, and the brains fail to register.

There are, by the way, 7 Fs in the sentence.

There's a blind spot here, not in the retinas or lenses but in the part of the mind that processes what the eyes are seeing. What you've got is a piece of bad mental programming. It takes reprogramming just to see what's in front of your eyes.

Scotoma is the medical terminology for blind spot. I never cease to be amazed by our scotomas, and how many we have. If we miss the Fs in that silly sentence, just imagine what we're not seeing in the rest of the world.

How many scotomas do you have in your professional life? Scotomas are especially hard to see because they blind you. They're everywhere. Real estate people, are you aware that 20 percent of the people in America are moving? Do you know who they are and where they are? You ought to, because they need your services, to sell the home they're leaving and find another one. They are all around you, and probably looking for you. Opportunities like this are everywhere, in every field. Unfortunately, though, there are as many scotomas as opportunities.

To paraphrase Abraham Lincoln, we've got to learn to think anew, in order to see anew. It works the other way, too. If you're seeing more clearly, you can think more clearly. Jesus said that before you look for the speck in your neighbor's eye you've got to take the log out of your own eye.

You've got to see to sell.

It's time for the next eye test, which I owe to my friend Larry Wilson, the Father of Counselor Selling. This is an old one but a good one. You might want to try it on your friends.

Nine Dots Puzzle

The object here is to connect all nine dots by drawing four lines, without lifting the pen or pencil from the paper. Give this a few minutes before you turn to the answer, which is on page 28.

Did you get it?

Most people don't, because they can't get out of the box the dots seem to make.

But nobody said anything about staying in the box, did they?

In point of fact, there isn't a box, just the **idea** of a box. But the idea is enough to keep you from solving the puzzle. This illustrates a different kind of scotoma, which is caused by seeing things that **aren't** there, which keep you from understanding what is there.

In either case the problem is self-programming.

The nine-dot puzzle also shows us something bigger than a mere blind spot. When we see something that isn't there, it's usually something like a box, which keeps us **in** something when we need or want to get **out**. Or vice versa. Somewhere deep down we believe in boxes and walls and all manner of restrictions and barriers and taboos. But, like the nine dots and four lines, most of life's puzzles can't be solved until we get out of the box.

What's true about seeing is true about every kind of input. We're selectively hard of hearing — tuning out, without knowing we're doing it, immensely valuable information. The problem is sometimes more like dyslexia. We read important information without absorbing it, and thinking about how it can apply to us. And all the while we're scared of the big, bad boxes that tell us how come we can't get from here to there, or do anything different from the way it's always been done.

Later chapters in this first section will be about new ways to learn from and use your own experience. Your own day-to-day data stream can teach you most of what you need to know for success, however you want to define success. The things we need are all around us. Most of the time they're looking for us! But we don't see them — just like we don't see all the Fs in the puzzle back on page 25. All the while we're seeing "You can't do this" boxes and walls.

You can't do new things until you learn to experience,

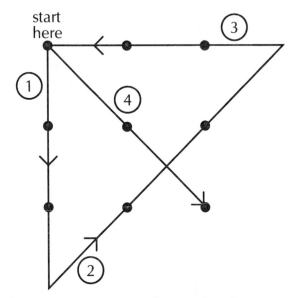

Nine Dots Puzzle Solution

and think about experience, in a new way. Frank Gilbreath, whose story was celebrated in **Cheaper By The Dozen**, revolutionized an industrial process that hadn't changed much in 5,000 years, just by taking a new look at it. Since the beginnings of civilization, brick-making involved 17 steps, from raw material to finished product. Gilbreath opened his eyes and cut the steps down to 5. By simplifying the process, he made bricks with 72 percent less effort, and a 191 percent increase in output-per-hour!

ACTION PLAN

New Eyes

• Do something to make the world seem different. Charles Dorane, a top-performing broker at Merrill-Lynch and one of our clients, suggests rearranging your office furniture. Drive to work by a new route. Go to lunch at a different time. Invite somebody you especially admire — a solid winner — to lunch. Stay away from those who want to talk you down, and slow you down, and drag you down. You know who they are. Stay away from the turkeys!

• Building on the freshness of your break in routine, spend a day on the job as if everything were brand new to you, seeing/hearing everything as if it's the first time.

• Any surprises? Write down the biggest one.

_____

_____

• Keep looking until you see some opportunities to expand your productivity/profit/efficiency, or however you define success. Write down the best opportunity.

_____

_____

• What kept you from seeing it before?

_____

_____

• Now that you're seeing it, what do you intend to **do** about it?

_____

_____

Out of the Box

• Treat yourself to a lunch where the powerful and influen-

tial — the men and women you'd most like to meet and do business with — dine.

• Order exactly what you want. This is education, not self-
indulgence.

• Look carefully around the restaurant, or club. Try to see
the barriers between you and the men and women around you.

• There aren't any, except the barriers in your head, your
own limiting thoughts.

• With your new, wide-open eyes, try to see all the restric-
tive boxes and restrictions and barriers that govern your aspirations and your life.

• Who walled you in? How?

_____

_____

• What's your plan to free yourself?

_____

_____

• How are you going to stay free?

_____

_____

Pop Quiz

One question, counts for 100 percent of the score.

• Will you, from now on, every day, absorb and think about
what's happening as if it's all new and exciting, with a special lookout for unnoticed opportunities?

_____

_____

The only correct answer is **YES!** If you get it wrong, sit in
brighter light and read this section again.

Booting Up

You can probably tell, by the way I've been using computer talk, that I am something less than an expert. The main lesson I've learned is that the best way to get your money's worth out of computers is to work with somebody energetic and smart who was born after 1960. I've got some of them around here.

One of the few specifics I know, on the subject of computers, is that it's very important to type in the right things after you turn the machine on. If you don't, you might as well not turn it on, because it isn't going to do anything useful. Between off and on a computer spends a few seconds "booting up." Then it wants to know what you want it to do.

You wake up in the morning in much the same manner. After sleeping, the consciousness goes from "off" to "on," and then there's a few minutes when the mind is fantastically receptive to instructions. This can be your **Golden Moment,** your **Sweet Spot,** if you tell yourself the right things.

Here's what I say to myself —

I'm healthy!

I'm wealthy!

I'm happy!

I get what I want because I deserve it, and

I DO WHAT I OUGHT TO DO, WHEN I OUGHT TO DO IT, WHETHER I WANT TO OR NOT.

NO DEBATE!

Try saying it to yourself right now. Out loud, if there's nobody else around. And don't just say it, **believe** it.

The other thing I know about a computer, besides that it's important to tell it the right things after you boot up, is the button you push when you're in deep trouble and don't know how to get out.

The button is called "Reset." It makes the machine drop what-

ever it's doing, forget all about it, and go back to where you started, ready to receive new instructions. What you're doing, my digi-
talized friends tell me, is "rebooting" the machine, so you've got a
clean start. "Reset" will get you out of almost any kind of trouble.

Here's a "Reset" button for the brain. You can push it whenever
you're in a frame of mind that you need to get out of.

Take a deep, slow breath.

Hold the breath for a moment.

Smile.

Feels good, doesn't it?

You've started the day all over again.

No Such Thing As A Silent Doubt

Cut out page 33, the one with the funny-looking numbers on it,
and then cut out each of the ten squares. Put the squares in a pile,
so the edges all line up. Do it all very carefully, as if you're going to
be graded on neatness.

The no-brainer activity gives us a few minutes to listen in on
our inner voices, the ones that talk at a rate of 2,000 words a
minute and never shut up.

What are yours saying?

If you're like most people, the brain-chatter is appalling.

One little voice says:

• Hey, I wonder what the numbers are for? This ought to be
really interesting.

Eight or nine others attack the enthusiastic voice:

• What does this have to do with marketing?

• I'm sick of this feel-good stuff. You get pumped up for a
couple days and then *pfffft,* nothing.

• This is boring. I should have bought the new Madonna
biography.

• No, I am not going to look for the stupid scissors.

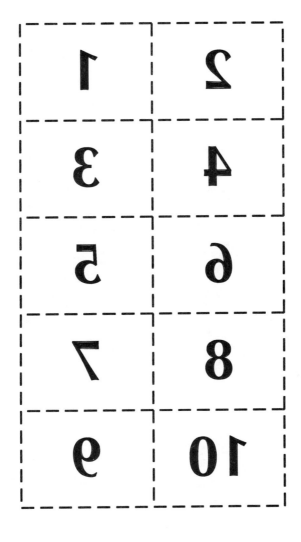

Meanwhile there's another 600 brain gremlins talking about everything bad that's happened since you were two years old, and everything bad that could possibly happen next. Other voices are telling you what's wrong with you, probably calling you names.

Played on loudspeakers, self-talk would sound as mean and discouraging as the Hallelujah Chorus is joyful and uplifting. If self-talk were a 100-channel cable TV system, only 16 channels would be positive and worth tuning in. The other 84 would be negative.

Psychologists say that you can never entirely silence the inner voices that talk you down. You can, however, learn to ignore them, quit believing what they say, and drown them out with positive self-talk.

Listening to your self-talk, and getting control of it, is a necessary first step toward success in selling, or any other kind of person-to-person interaction.

Why bother with the voices inside your head, if nobody else knows what they're saying?

• The secret about inner voices, which very few people appreciate, is that they're not really **inner**. Other folks can tell what they're saying. Maybe not in detail, but everybody knows the gist.

No, we're not talking about mind-reading and witchcraft. The give-away is the nine-tenths of communication which is **not** verbal. Body language, one way or the other, will say whatever it is you're trying so hard not to say.

There is no such thing as a silent doubt!

If you doubt yourself or what you're doing, other people will share your same doubts. Doubters are not going to tell you "Yes, I'll take it!" A sales career built on doubt is like the biblical house built on sand — it cannot stand. Persuasion must be built on the rock of confidence.

Three kinds of confidence are absolutely critical. We call them the Three Ps.

Persuasive Success

Profession

Person   Process

3 Ps – The kinds of confidence on which persuasion or selling <u>must</u> stand.

• **P**erson. Confidence in your own integrity and unique value as a person.

• **P**rofession. Confidence in the value of the contribution to society you're making, by doing your job well, along with confidence that the product, service or idea you represent is a good one, and will benefit buyers.

• **P**rocess. Confidence that you have communicative techniques and a selling system that will produce positive results in all respects.

Selling stands on these three principles, the way a tripod stands. Kick out one of the legs, and the whole business falls over.

This book takes care of the third P. The NEER system, our subject-matter, is a beginning-to-end Process for making the contacts you most need to make to build your business. You'll meet more qualified, less resistant buyers more often and more easily — with less effort and emotional stress. If NEER doesn't do wonders for your performance and confidence, as it has done for thousands of our clients, you need more than what we at Planned Marketing Associates are qualified to give you.

Before Process, though, come the first two **P**s. Number One, **P**ersonal confidence, is a baseline requirement for success. When a customer says "I'll take it," he or she is really saying "I'll take **you**." This cannot happen until that other person **believes** you, **likes** you, and **trusts** you. I call the critical acceptance-factor **BLT**. And no matter how well you can play-act, you're not going to establish BLT until you really believe in, and like, and trust, yourself. Others cannot respect you until you respect yourself.

This is why you have to start listening to and controlling self-destructive self-talk. You'll have to work at it. If you don't, negativity happens, all by itself. In this respect, negativity is like poverty. Do nothing and it just happens. It doesn't require a plan.

If you don't do something about the noisy enemies in your own head, they'll always be telling everybody about you, louder than you can talk.

It is an absolute truth that whatever you are giving out is coming back to you. As ye sow, so shall ye reap — the law of reciprocity is the most important guiding principal in business, and life in general.

Self-esteem, by itself, won't get you to success in business persuasion. A self-esteem boost, without substantive, systematized training, is like one of those coffee-and-glazed donut breakfasts. You're hyper for a little bit, but then you crash, lower than where you started. On the other hand, no amount of persuasive technique and system can compensate for a low opinion of yourself.

ACTION PLAN

The Number On Your Forehead

Now you can do something with the numbers I asked you to cut out. One of them will be the life score you give yourself. Remember Charlie? When we first met him he had a big bright **9.** After he went down in flames, he had **4**, tops, which is too low to sustain life as anybody would want to live it. (In my lowest moments, I've been a **4** myself. **4s** don't like to be around other **4s**. They'd rather have **3s** and **2s** around, to pick on.)

Exercise A:
  • Take the numbers into the bathroom or bedroom or wherever there's a big, well-lit mirror.
  • Try the numbers on, one by one. Take a good look at yourself with each number.
  • Which one fits?

- Is this the number you really want to wear? If not, why not?

_____

_____

- **10s** can quit reading here, and start writing their own books.
- Hold the **9** to your forehead.
- It's really you, isn't it?
- No, this isn't pretending. You are a **9**. Less than perfect, but plenty good enough to feel great about yourself, which is the way others feel about you, too.
- Carry your **9**, so it's always with you. When you feel yourself losing points, sneak a look at yourself, wearing your number.

Keeping Your Number High

Healthy self-esteem is, of course, more than a number, and achieving it can be a difficult, lengthy process. In this book, which is about my marketing system, I can't begin to do justice to serious and persistent self-image problems, which are rightfully in the realm of clinical psychology.

My own experience suggests that loss of self-esteem on the job has two main causes:

A) Not taking responsibility for things within your control, which you can do **something** about.

B) Taking responsibility for things outside your control, which you can do **nothing** about.

Both are prescriptions for needless self-blame.

If you've been giving yourself a low life score, raise it by:

1) **Accepting** yourself and the things you cannot change.

2) **Looking** inside yourself for your feelings of self worth. The approval of others can be an addiction. Kick the habit, and earn your own approval.

3) **Concentrating** on your strengths — not your weaknesses.

4) **Remembering** you don't need to be perfect.

5) **Doing** things that you enjoy.

6) **Trying** something new on a regular basis. Take some risks. Learn to grow.

7) **Finding** mentors, to learn from and emulate. Heroes in your own life give hope and something to strive for.

Exercise B:

Do some inside work on raising your forehead number:

• Write down something that bothers you, which is really your responsibility, which you could do something about.

_____

_____

• What are you going to do about it?

_____

_____

• Starting when?

_____

_____

• Change the last answer to **now.**

• Write down something that troubles you, which is not your responsibility, which you can't do a thing about.

_____

_____

• Think about what you just wrote down, and say these words, "To heck with it," or equivalent thereof. (If you need to be more forceful and profane, go for it.)

• Mean what you just said.

Just A Salesman?

For some sellers, the second of the three Ps — belief in the value and integrity of one's own profession — is the shakiest. Many of us, even though we make our livings selling, have a prejudice against sales — as if the business that makes the economic world go around is something to be ashamed of!

My own definition of shame is a belief that developed before you knew it was being developed. This "less-than" attitude about selling fits the bill exactly. A lot of people grew up hearing their parents and family friends talking down salespeople. "Tell her I'm not in, she's **just** a salesperson." "Oh, he's **just** an account rep." As if they're selling **just** because they don't have whatever it took to make it in administration, finance, production, or, better yet, one of the classic professions — doctor, lawyer, orthodontist — that everybody's mama daydreams about.

I guess I was lucky, in terms of early attitude-formation. I did, indeed, hear jokes about salesmen, from the immediate family, but I also saw how well my Uncle George Jordan and Uncle Barney Vanston were doing. They both sold insurance. Other people's jokes didn't take the shine off my uncles' big, black Cadillacs and city clothes and — most of all — the freedom to come and go and set their own limits, work their own hours. I couldn't help but notice that the folks laughing at them were working themselves half to death on farms!

I owe a lot to my rural upbringing. On a farm, you grow up working. My father showed me the value of hard work, and how to manage.

The farm itself gave me something to work for — getting **off** the farm.

And Uncle George and Uncle Barney showed me the way.

This, I guess, is why I never developed an attitude problem about selling.

Take a look at your own attitude. This is especially important if you just got out of college. Higher educators — the same folks who forgot to teach you anything about thinking — have an attitude problem, vis-à-vis selling, which can't help but rub off. Very few professors will say to their best and brightest students, "You ought to be in sales." Only about 7 percent of college students identify sales as their career goal. And I know of only a few business schools that offer courses in Persuasion, even though their graduates' ultimate success — in any field — will depend on their persuasive powers! Studies have shown that 85 percent of business successes are owed to people skills, which are virtually ignored at colleges and universities!

Up in the ivory tower, behind those ivied walls, you can get the notion that the ultimate business challenges and rewards lie in areas other than selling.

Wrong. This couldn't be more wrong.

• Of the 10 top-paid professions in the United States, half are sales positions.

• Selling is the only profession that has no limits, other than what you set for yourself.

• Selling, unlike more structured fields, confers total personal liberty, and total personal responsibility. You can work as hard, or as little, make as much, or as little, as you want.

• Without sales, nobody else has a job. More and more corporate leaders are recognizing this fundamental business truth and making it **everybody's** job to make and keep customers, which is what salespeople have always done.

The greatest leaders and discoverers in history have all been powerful sellers. If they hadn't persuaded somebody else to pay attention and say "Yes!" we never would have heard of them, and the world wouldn't be what it is.

When I think about gung-ho sellers, I always think of Christopher Columbus. This guy persuaded one of the most powerful monarchs in the world to put money into sending three very expensive ships to what seemed to be certain destruction. Columbus went to five kings with his flip chart presentation. What did they tell him? **NO.** Queen Isabella finally said yes. This, I think, says a lot about the sound business instincts of women, which males until recently have been trying to deny. It also says a great deal about Columbus' persuasive gifts. But his biggest sale wasn't the Queen. He joined the Immortal Salesmen Of All Time when he talked his crews into joint venturing with him and **then** talked them out of turning back, even though turning back looked like the only way to save their lives.

"Stay the course," the way Columbus said it, had more selling power than "Coke is it!" He was a great navigator, for sure, but if he hadn't sold as well as he sailed we'd still be in the Old Country, and I wouldn't be talking with a Texas accent.

What about Benjamin Franklin? He must have had a presentation, and a close every bit as good as Columbus'. This guy got 55 other people to sign up for a deal — Independence — that hadn't ever been tried and, if it didn't work, was a near certain death sentence. When you think about old Ben, don't just think of the brilliant things he said — think about what he did. He **sold**.

Without the power of persuasion — selling — we'd still be digging for bugs to eat with sharp sticks. No great human advancement can occur until someone sells the concept and someone else says, "Yes, I'll take it!"

Your First, Most Important, Sale

After I graduated from the University of Texas, I went to work selling Light Crust Flour for Burrus Mills.

Among the premium brands, flour is pretty much flour. But I never had any doubt that Light Crust was the best. I was convinced it was so good you could eat it with a spoon. Even now, I get excited just thinking about that flour.

Of course flour, all by itself, wouldn't have gotten me or anybody else worked up. But our flour didn't come by itself. It had a special aura about it. Our company was Texas-based, and sponsored a country band, with its own radio show. You didn't get just fluffy biscuits or flaky pie with Light Crust — you got music to eat them by. This was a hard combination to beat, sitting there in a country kitchen, with a hot biscuit and melting butter on it, maybe a little honey, bacon frying, and the Light Crust Dough Boys doing "San Antonio Rose" on the radio. It's been 30 years, but it all comes back.

I always knew Light Crust was the best buy for the grocers, even when the competition beat our prices.

I can still hear one old guy in Louisiana telling me "Hey Boy, I can get Gold Medal Flour for 41 cents a bag. And you're getting 50 cents!"

"How much does that Gold Medal salesman get for Light Crust flour?" I asked him.

"He ain't got Light Crust! What kind of stuff you givin' me?"

"This isn't stuff," I said. "That other guy doesn't sell Light Crust — I do!"

I was grinning at him now. "And if you don't get Light Crust, you don't get **me!**"

I must have been grinning just right, because he didn't do me bodily harm. He yelled a dirty word at me, like he wanted to.

But then he bought my flour, a lot of it.

Of course it wasn't a grin that sealed that deal. And when I said **me,** I wasn't talking about the pleasure of my company. I meant — and he knew I meant — that nobody else would do as much to help him sell the flour and build his business. Every time I went to his store, I took him an idea that could help him. I taught him and his people how to sell. I put on special promotions. The people who came into the store for my weekend shindigs weren't just buying more Light Crust. They were buying more of everything he sold.

The 9 cents extra per bag, over Gold Medal, didn't matter because he got more than 9 cents a bag in extra **value.** Light Crust was, really and truly, the best flour deal he could get.

Knowing that value was on my side, and working hard to make sure it stayed on my side, made me a successful seller. Without that, I couldn't have risen above the mediocre. No one can.

Unless you're a natural-born grifter and con-artist, devoid of conscience, you must absolutely **know** that what you're selling has benefits for the customer equal to or greater than the price you're asking for it.

Your own sense of personal integrity depends on your sense of the value of the product, service or idea you represent.

STOP!
LOOK!
LISTEN!
WITHOUT VALUE
AND INTEGRITY
NOTHING **WORKS!**

Make your first, most complete, most convincing presentation to yourself. Until you've said "Yes!" convincing other people to say it will be a thankless, uphill battle.

Remember that value is a complex formula that figures in all of your product's relative advantages.

• Value is much more than quality. It has to be, with so many good products on the market, and government safeguards against shoddiness and fraud.

• Value is more than a competitive price.

• Value is everything you and your company do to help the customer get the most from your product, service or idea.

• An edge in quality, or conspicuous savings, can land a first-time customer. But repeat sales are founded on what you do to make sure the customer gets the greatest continuing benefits. Your selling career depends on repeat business.

• Value doesn't mean value to **you**, but to the customer. Always look at value from the other person's point-of-view.

Written out in black-and-white, this all seems pretty obvious. But most salespeople have never convinced themselves of the baseline value of their product, and their own integrity, before they start trying to convince other people.

Most of the time the result of a long, hard look at your product's value is a surprise — a very pleasant one. What you're selling is probably better than you thought. But then again this shouldn't be a surprise, should it? Chances are your company has been in business for a long time. If it didn't offer good value, the customers would have quit buying long ago.

ACTION PLAN

It's A Wonderful Life

Remember that glorious old movie, *It's A Wonderful Life*, where the angel shows Jimmy Stewart how the world would be without him?

You get to be the angel in your own re-make, which is about your customers' world — if the product or service you provide were to suddenly disappear. For example, if you sell FAX machines, the world is without FAX machines, of all brands. Nobody has conceived of such a thing.

• Are your customers' lives easier or harder? Explain

_____

_____

_____

_____

_____

• They're not spending money on what you sell. But is the absence of it **costing** them money? What about extra time and effort?

_____

_____

_____

• Would their lives and productivity be improved if what you sell were suddenly introduced? How so?

_____

_____

_____

_____

• Would it be worth the price?

_____

_____

• If you appeared in this imaginary world with your product or service, would the customers get excited about it?

_____

_____

• You ought to be just as excited about the product, service or idea you represent as your make-believe people.

• **Be** as excited as you ought to be!

**The sale happens at the moment when
the buyer recognizes value and the seller
recognizes commitment!**

Get In Before You Get Out

Most of you just gave a resounding "Yes!" to what you're selling. But a few had to say "No."

This happens in our Power of Persuasion seminars, too. Once in a while participants come to the inescapable conclusion that they don't believe in what they're doing. They cannot, no matter what they do, get excited about the product, service or idea they represent.

If this is actually the problem, a job change is the only remedy.

But it's much too early to come to any such conclusion.

Changing the way you **do** your job — this is the job change that most people really need.

After the most discouraging night in my selling career, when the pig farmer in East Texas said "No" seven times and my ego was declared a total loss, I went to an older and much more successful businessman. I called him my coach. I wasn't using the word "mentor" yet, but that's what he really was.

I told him I couldn't take it any more. I was going to get out of the insurance business.

"You can't," he told me.

"Of course I can get out of the insurance business."

"No you can't," he said.

"What are you talking about?" I said.

"You can't get out of the insurance business," he told me, "because you ain't never been **in** it."

I got ready to argue some more, but then stopped, because I knew he was right. I asked him what I should do.

Buy *Think and Grow Rich* by Napoleon Hill, he said. Then read it and start living by it. He said I should go out and get my own copy because if he gave me one I wouldn't read it, much less take it to heart.

I replay that scene, which changed my life, whenever somebody comes to me and talks about needing to quit and find a new job.

I tell them that they've already got a new job, which is their old job enhanced with new commitment and enthusiasm and the techniques of NEER.

I ask them to give it everything they've got, for 90 days. I'm asking you the same thing.

You can't get out of anything until you've been in it.

So get in!

Make a firm resolution to work with total enthusiasm, applying what you learn in this book. Don't wait for your company to do more for you, before you'll do more for it. People who wait for more rewards before they'll work more remind me of the man who came in out of the snow and said to his stove, "I'll give you some wood, but first you've got to give me some heat." What happened? He froze to death, looking at a cold, dark stove.

When you really stoke up a stove, it gives off more than heat. It gives off light, too, a wonderful cherry-red glow. If you start stoking up your job, it'll glow too. The glow is fun. Work, when you really give it everything, isn't work anymore. It's more like playing.

This, by the way, is one of the secrets of the ultra-successful. They're working day and night because working, for them, is a lot more fun than golf or water skiing. There's nothing they'd rather be doing.

> **If not now, when?**
> **If not here, where?**

ACTION PLAN

No Trial, No Jury

Make a commitment to use the principles and techniques set forth in this book for at least 21 days, before you even **think** about making a judgment about them and their applicability to you.

If you don't come to the trial, you can't sit on the jury.

Since there's too much here to try everything at once, we ask that you start with a half-dozen specifics that seem to be most immediately useful to you, and put them into practice for 21 consecutive days. Building on that core with other components of the NEER system will come naturally.

The trial period, 21 days, is the time psychologists say it takes to form a **habit**. Once a new way of thinking or working is habit, it's all yours, automatically. The first good habits are a solid foundation for more habit-building.

Saying **Yes, I commit** to a book isn't enough. Your commitment should be made in public, in front of others. Witness signatures on the following Statement of Solemn Intent are just as important as your own.

I, _____ (Your Name), do solemnly swear, in front of myself and two witnesses, to implement no fewer than 5 NEER principles and techniques in this book, for 21 consecutive days. An interruption in the program will require me to start from Day 1, until I reach 21.

If I have a spouse or fiancè, he or she must be one of the signatories. I am required to give periodic progress reports to this loved-one.

If the first 21-day program brings greater success and satisfaction, I commit to adapt another 5 or more NEER components to my own situation for 21 days. As long as this system brings improvement, I'll keep adding new components of NEER and making them habits.

Before my periods of commitment are over, I will refrain from making negative judgments about NEER, or its potential for me.

Signed and Sworn this _____ (date)

_____(Your signature)

Witness 1: _____

Witness 2: _____

The NEER™ SYSTEM is not on trial — I am!

2

80/20 — The Best Juice with the Best Prospects

MAGIC NUMBERS

I have always held it is better to copy genius than to create mediocrity. We can put the rest of humanity to work for us, so we don't have to rediscover what has already been discovered. One of the beautiful things about using other people's knowledge and accomplishments is that we don't always have to understand what makes the stuff work — as long as we know for sure that it does work.

I personally don't have a clue about how come Mr. or Ms. State Trooper can point the radar gun at my particular Ford Motor Company product and know how fast I'm going. The trooper doesn't know either. But somewhere there are these folks with plastic pocket protectors who know all the magic numbers about radar, who designed a machine so the trooper can tell if I'm going 78 mph on I-10 because I don't want to miss the plane to the West Coast.

Fortunately I've got my own R&D and electrical engineering staff. I've never actually met them, but I know they're good, because they built this little black box that sits on the dashboard and squawks before old Smoky can get me on his radar. Life is full of magic numbers, which we don't know, which are the operating principles of useful things we don't understand. Nevertheless, we use them every day. The numbers, of course, aren't really magic — people have labored for years, sometimes hundreds and thousands of years, to understand them. But to the rest of us they might as well be magic. Without knowing a thing about aerodynamics, I can pretty well count on the 6:05 plane getting me to California.

We can't afford to be so complacent in our own businesses. This is because we're the pilots. And in sales you don't just, figuratively speaking, fly. You navigate, design and build your own flying machine, from scratch. (When you're really doing your job you also serve the orange juice and champagne!) The difference between cruising altitude and a belly landing is how well you've mastered the underlying principles of your profession. You've got to know your magic numbers.

80/20 is as basic to sellers — indeed, to all aspects of business — as the Doppler effect to the radar guys and the principle of lift to the engineers at Boeing.

80/20 is a ratio, 80 percent to 20 percent, four to one.

Broadly speaking, it means that at least 80 percent of the output comes from 20 percent of the input, whatever the output and input are.

In terms of your work, 80/20 means that at least one-fifth of what you do yields at least four-fifths of the desired results — in volume, commission or however you measure success.

Whether or not you've looked at your 80/20, or if you don't even **believe** there is such a thing, 80/20 is there, working for you — or against you — all day, every day. You can't escape it any more than you can escape the Law of Gravity.

The work/results ratio is only one of the 80/20s making your universe go around, which you must track and understand.

• In your company, 20 percent of the employees do at least 80 percent of the business.

• Among customers — yours, your company's and the industry's — 20 percent are responsible for at least 80 percent of the orders. 80/20 works large and small, frontwards and back-wards. It works for the downside, as well as the upside:

• At least 80 percent of your problems are coming from 20 percent of your clients, who are **not** in the golden 20 percent that yield 80 percent or more of your successes.

All of this is of more than academic interest. Understanding the 80/20s will show you:

• **WHO** to call on, and who **not** to call on

• **WHAT** you should do **more**, and what you should do **less**, or quit doing altogether

• **WHEN** your activities are most fruitful

• **WHERE** effort is best spent

• **WHY** all of the above is true

What we've got here are journalism's famous Five Ws, for telling a news story. With 80/20 you can write yourself a story about your career as it is today and what you need to do to reach your goals.

The goal of 80/20 **is** 80/20. By applying the simple principle of putting your best efforts where they'll do the most, and sparing yourself misspent effort, you can join the 20 percent of sellers who do 80 percent of business, and garner 80 percent of the rewards. If you're already in this top one-fifth, you can aim for its top 20 percent, the elite's elite.

The First 80/20: Your Best Customers

One of the ways you can tell if you're doing things right is that people get irritated with you. Of course they also get that way when you're doing things wrong, or not doing anything at all. But these are different kinds of mad than the kind that comes with success, which has this unmistakable green, envious tint to it. Once you've had a few successes, it's easy to recognize.

One of the executives at my insurance company was feeling a little scratchy when I first took over the company. Maybe it annoyed him to be bought out by somebody so much shorter than he was. He **had** to have an argument with me before we could start getting along. Pretty soon he found something to argue about. It was not, naturally, what was really bothering him, but that didn't matter. In this respect, offices are like marriages. When the urge to dispute gets strong, any old subject will do.

The guy argued with me about 80/20.

He was telling me about the 8,000 policy holders he had.

"Betcha about 1,600 of those policy holders do 80 percent of the business," I said.

"No way!" he said, a little more aggressively than he needed to.

"You ought to take a look," I said.

"No way!"

"Check it out," I said, "and bring me a report." When you can say things like this, you don't need to raise your voice.

Some time later he came back and threw down his report. "You were wrong!" he said.

"No way!" This time I was yelling.

Then he explained to me how wrong I was:

He didn't find any 1,600 customers doing 80 percent of the business. He found **800 who were doing 90 percent!**

Remember that 80/20 says **at least** 80 percent of the output comes from 20 percent of the input. Real-world business often shows a much more dramatic imbalance. I have observed, in many situations, that 5 percent of the people are doing 95 percent of the business.

But this fellow needed to be right more than I did, so I let it go. He didn't want to argue any more, anyway. He was too fired-up about changing his part of the operation, based on what these new numbers were telling him. And he did, indeed, make some very big changes. He concentrated his people's efforts on servicing the best customers. He looked at the common denominators of those best customers, and went to work finding prospects that fit the profile.

He turned his 80/20 around and looked at his customer base again. This time he was looking for trouble spots. Guess what? He found 1,600 customers who were causing, by far, most of the problems. None of them belonged to the top 1,600. Many of them were, in fact, costing the company more money in service than we were making from them. They were, literally, more trouble than they were worth. When he saw the numbers that guy — who had been so anxious to prove me wrong about 80/20 — let the problem customers go. In so doing, he saved the company something like $50,000. He saved time and energy, which he and staff put to much better use, servicing and prospecting prime customers. And he saved everybody a whole lot of headaches.

This story shows what 80/20 can do, when you get it on your side. And we were only working with the first of the three 80/20s we emphasize in the Planned Marketing seminars. Used with the others, the benefits do more than add up — they multiply.

I never cease to be amazed at how many sales professionals have never taken a close, analytical look at their client bases, to see where their action really is. Most people have been taught about 80/20, in one form or another. There is, however, an enormous

distance between:
- **hearing** about something
- **knowing** it
- **knowing** what you ought to **do** about it
- and **DOING** it!

Ideas have to get out of our heads, and into action, before they do anybody any good.

ACTION PLAN

Finding Your First 80/20

For this exercise you'll need a list of your customers, and the business provided by each, for last year, or this year through the most recent quarter, the closer to the present the better. (If you keep records the way you ought to, you'll have everything tallied up to this minute.)

- Using the sample on page 59 as a model, split a blank piece of paper into two vertical columns. Label the left-hand column "Customers" and the right side "Business." This will be your 80/20 Customer Tally Sheet.

- Total **all** the business you generated in the period you're about to chart. Measure your business in the way that makes the most sense to you. For sellers this is usually commissions or total sales, in dollars. In certain cases the best measure might be units of product moved to the customers.

- Multiply the above total of your business by .80. (In case you've forgotten all your arithmetic, this is the same as subtracting a fifth from the total, so four-fifths are left.)

- Write the name of your biggest customer on the left-hand side of your tally sheet. Put the business the customer generates on the right. Below number one, make the same entries for the number two customer. Below that, number three, and so on.

80/20 CUSTOMER TALLY SHEET

Total Business Dollars	$66,966
	x .80
80% of Total Business	$53,573

CUSTOMERS	BUSINESS
1. ADCO Inc.	16,243
2. FounDeCo.	11,414
3. ELJ Inc.	10,721
4. Grimes Distributors	5,802
5. Mesa Corp.	3,382
6. Diana Designs	2,601
7. Lopez & Lopez	1,472
8. Cayon Mfg.	1,017
9. Feldman Construction	921
Total (= 80% of all business)	$53,573

Total Client Base	= 45 clients
9 Clients	= 20% of client base

20% of clients = 80% of business!

• Keep adding this list of customers, in descending order of the business they do with you, and keep a running total of the business they all do with you, combined.

• You can stop when the running total equals 80 percent of all your business.

• How many clients account for 80 percent of your business?_____ What percentage of your total client base is represented here? _____

• Any surprises? Explain

_____

_____

• Take a long, appreciative look at the clients you've listed. You might want to give them a name. Preferred Customer List, Gold Club Members, Platinum Circle, whatever. These are the most important individuals in your selling life. From here on out, you'll want to pay the closest possible attention to them, and learn everything about them you can.

• Keep this first 80/20 tally sheet handy. You'll need it for the rest of this chapter. You will, actually, need it — in updated form — for the rest of your working life.

Vital Signs

The importance of the first 80/20, which you just worked out, is that it provides a simple diagnostic tool, which allows you to make some informed judgments about your business.

Every profession — from brain surgery to auto mechanics — has its diagnostics, which are easy-to-read indicators that tell about very complicated things. These days hospitals can do 3-D computer scans of brains. They've got surgeons who can saw holes in the skull and look for themselves, and show you videotapes afterwards. But if you bang yourself on the head, and go to the emergency room to make sure it wasn't serious, nobody starts scanning and cutting. They do some old-time basics. They take your pulse and blood pressure, ask you if you know who you are and where you are and what day it is. These simple indicators, called "vital signs," speak volumes to the medical staff.

The 80/20s and a few other diagnostics this book teaches will tell you your **business vital signs.**

A broker friend of ours started giving free investments seminars, as a way of attracting prospects. His turnout was consistently good. He had, it seemed, found himself a very effective means of reaching potential clients. Just by showing up, they seemed to be pre-qualifying themselves. Anybody interested enough to listen to a talk ought to be plenty interested in **buying** what the talk is about.

So it would seem. But his seminars weren't doing much for sales. Wanting to know why not, our friend did an 80/20 analysis of his client base, like the one you just did of yours. He found that he made most of his money from top executives, doing portfolio planning. But the people who came to his programs didn't have the financial clout his best customers had. With 80/20, he found out that the seminars did not bring him the reach he really needed. He needed more customers like his best customers. And his best customers were not coming to his seminars.

In fisherman's terms, he was casting for rainbow trout in a pond stocked with crappies and perch. He could try different baits **forever,** and **never** catch what he was fishing for!

Selling, most of the time, isn't quite so black-and-white. No matter how you prospect, if you keep at it, the law of averages will get you a customer. Maybe a few customers. But never enough to do more than survive (if you're lucky enough to get that many). Successful sellers, and successful people in general, get the law of averages working for them.

80/20 is a way to saddle-break the law of averages, so you can ride it to where you want to go.

Remember this:

• All customers may have been **created** equal, but that was a long time before they grew up and started doing business with you. Some of them are a lot more equal than others, and deserve more time and attention. Extra effort here will be more than paid back.

• Prospects aren't any more equal than the customers are. The best prospects are, in most cases, those that most resemble your best customers.

Nobody I know of is more acquainted with Hailey's Law of Customer **In**equality than automobile salesmen. Lately we've been working with several large dealer systems, teaching the sellers how to get out of the showroom, to where their best prospects are. The time when you could make a nice living from "ups" (car dealer talk for folks who walk into the showroom) is long gone. It's never coming back. Pro-active market development is the only way to go.

The "ups" making the rounds these days are very likely to be the **least** qualified prospects, who are coming into the showroom because all the other dealers turned them down for financing. Smart, qualified car shoppers are relying less and less on the traditional tire kicking and test driving to reach their buying decisions. A salesperson whose scope is limited to his selling floor may not be seeing his best prospects, much less selling to them. To make sales, you've got to identify the customers at the high end of the 80/20, find out where they are and **reach** them.

ACTION PLAN

Targeting

• Look analytically at your 80/20 Customer Tally Sheet.

• What do your most productive customers have in common?

_____

_____

• From those commonalities, work up a best-customer profile, that includes the most important identifying factors.

_____

_____

_____

• Did you know, before now, where you were getting most of your business? What surprises you about the profile?

_____

_____

_____

• Where should you be looking for people who match the profile?

_____

_____

_____

• Write out an Action Plan to expand your business — by making more sales with your current best customers, and making **new sales** to prospects who are like the best customers.

_____

_____

_____

_____

More Surprises

If 80/20, so far, has raised your eyebrows, you'd better brace yourself. The next 80/20 might knock you out of your chair. The results, for most people, are downright shocking. Now that you've looked at the customers, it's time to examine yourself, and the things you do for 8 or 10 hours a day (or more) which are, supposedly, productive work.

Take careful note of the "supposedly" in the last sentence. It's important. We keep finding out, when we look at what people do all day, that "work" — meaning productive effort — takes up very little of the average "work" day. Offices are buzzing with everything **but** work — unproductive meetings, noncontributing conversations and coffee pot seminars, paper-shuffling, and on and on. We have found out, too, that most people can't tell the difference between real, productive work, and **make** work, or even **fake** work, because they've never examined the results of their activities.

Most people are too concerned about staying busy, or at least looking busy, without paying enough attention to yield.

ACTIVITY should NEVER be confused with ACCOMPLISHMENT!

My friend Rick Michaels, who finances broadcast media and cable system development, recently sold a radio station. Several months after the deal, the new owner called Tim Minowski, one of Rick's key people. The owner was in Charlie condition, an absolute wreck. The station was going bust, to the point that he was on the verge of losing it.

Tim was, naturally, surprised. This seemed like too short a time for such a major catastrophe. He flew up to see if he could help. Tim asked the new owner to look at his daybook, and exercise his memory, and write down everything he'd done, every day, since he took over the station. After the owner had logged his activities, Tim told him to put a dollar sign next to the activities that directly contributed to the station's bottom line.

There were, in that 45-day period, three things that earned a **$!** The rest of what he'd been doing brought in no money at all. The owner had been busy, but for all the good it did he could have rented Kung Fu movies and stayed at home.

That little bit of business diagnosis was enough to begin nursing his station back to health.

The truth is that most of us — literally — do not know what we're doing. If we do have some idea what we're doing — we don't have any idea what good it is doing us.

It is not enough to know who your juiciest customers are. You have to know where your own best juice is. You must know, in detail, **what** you are doing, **with whom** and **when**, and which of those things are bringing results.

This brings us to the second 80/20. When you take a look at what you do, on the job, you are looking at the same magic percentages.

• At least 80 percent of your success, however you define it, comes from 20 percent of what you do.

• Conversely, at least 20 percent of what you do contributes very little.

If you don't believe this, we're about to help you prove it to yourself.

ACTION PLAN

Self-Surveillance

• Starting tomorrow morning, begin following yourself through the workday. Keep a diary of what you do. You can use photocopies of the Daily Activity Log on page 66. Blank daybook pages also work well.

• Be precise about **when** the various activities begin and end. Each entry should clearly specify what you were doing, and with whom, on the phone, in person, etc.

DAILY ACTIVITY LOG

Name   Date

$\boxed{\$}$ = Revenue $\boxed{+}$ = Worthwhile $\boxed{O}$ = No Result $\boxed{-}$ = Counter
Producing   Productive

Time	With Whom	What	Where	Result

• Be **honest** and **merciless**. This is for you, and nobody else. If you spent 15 minutes in the break room flirting with a senior programmer analyst, and then shuffled papers for 20 minutes having adults-only daydreams, do not write down "2:05-2:20 conference with data processing. 2:20-2:40 reviewing July departmental reports."

• Don't let the fact that you are looking over your own shoulder radically alter what you do — not right away. At first this ought to be covert surveillance, as much as you can make it so. Kidding yourself will work against this or any other exercise in self-improvement.

• After a day, you can start scoring each activity for the benefit accrued. Use your own marking system, or something like this:

> **$** = Directly revenue producing. New sales, repeats, bigger orders, etc.
> **+** = Not directly revenue producing, but worthwhile. Prospecting, research, etc.
> **0** = Nada
> **-** = Counterproductive

A word or two explanation, particularly for $ and + entries — "new order..... wants to see product samples," etc. — adds a lot to the interpretive value.

• If you've been keeping "To-Do" lists and a thorough appointment book — if not, why not? — you can work backward through the past few weeks, while you gather new data on the job. Score the recent past the same way you're scoring the daily logs.

• What is your most productive activity? If the answer surprises you, say why.

_____

_____

• Are you doing as much productive work as you thought you were?

_____

• If you were your own boss, and knew everything you just found out, what sort of disciplinary action would you recommend?

_____

• Don't let the above two responses get you down. Practically everybody who starts an activity log is surprised — at the least — at how little of their time has been going to focused, directed, productive work.

• Keep looking. **What** produces most? **When** are the results best? **Where** are you having the most successes?

_____

_____

_____

• Work your **Ws** against each other, to look for interrelationships. Patterns will start jumping out right away. With a week or two of daily logs, it will become crystal clear that certain activities work best at certain times. Where your efforts are best spent also varies with time. Maybe calls on customers are most effective in the morning, phone contacts are best for the early afternoon, and that paperwork, necessary but not productive, should be relegated to the end of the day, when neither in-person contacts nor phoning is effective. Specifics vary, but the patterns are always there, governing your workday, whether you know it or not.

• Write out the most important patterns you've discovered, the **whens** and **wheres** of your key activities.

_____

_____

_____

_____

Daily Action Plan

Time	To Do	With Whom	Where	Result I Want

• Do your best stuff, with the best buyers at the best times in the best places.
• Do your bookwork and other necessities in the down times.

• Using what you've learned so far, fill out a make-believe, ideal daily log that has you doing your best stuff, at the best times, in the best places. Put necessary but non-producing tasks, paperwork and other things you have to do to keep your job in the day's low-yield periods.

• The ideal daily log is now tomorrow's **Daily Action Plan** (with, of course, adjustments for prior commitments).

• Any improvements?

_____

• It'll get even better.

• This sort of analysis doesn't always come easily. If you're really fighting it, this is a sign that you particularly need it. Ask for help from a friend or maybe your spouse.

Flying On Instruments

Either of the first two 80/20s shows you how to accomplish more with less time and effort. Both, side by side, are a double benefit. But the results begin to explode, with exponential increases, when you work them in combination.

With the 80/20s, you can put **your best juice with your best customers.**

Make your best moves with the best people at the best times in the best places — this is the formula for victory in any human endeavor. It explains how armies and athletes and companies overcome rivals who are larger and stronger, who — when you look at them on paper — shouldn't be able to lose. Generals have defeated much larger and better-armed foes by massing their best forces where the enemy is vulnerable, at the moment when they're especially vulnerable. Coaches and players of underdog teams recognize the other side's moments of vulnerability, turn them into moments of opportunity, and win.

It isn't always simple to marry what you now know about your best customers and prospects and your own effectiveness and the events of busy, often confusing, real-life workdays. The process takes imagination, willingness to try new approaches, flexibility. The 80/20s will, perhaps, make life seem a little more complicated. Very quickly, though, they'll make it all a lot simpler. When you get the hang of it, you'll see straight through what used to look like hopeless, blinding confusion.

Up to now you've been flying by the seat of your pants, but now you can know exactly where you're going, day or night, clear or cloudy. The 80/20s give you a set of reliable navigating instruments.

Using these percentages simplifies decision-making by giving criteria for making Yes-No decisions about **who** you ought to be spending time with, **what** you should be doing with them, **when** and **where.**

In our seminars, we talk about 80/20 to the Third Power: $80/20^3$ This is not math, so much as a way of reminding ourselves that a lot more good things happen when you **multiply** rather than **add** advantages. $80/20^3$ is also a shorthand way of saying that the first two 80/20s used together, will, inevitably, get you into the third 80/20, the top 20 percent in your company, your industry, and sellers in general.

The third 80/20 is much more than a target, though. It is a repository of information and years of experience that you can tap into, just by asking.

We recently trained the number one and number two sellers at an investments brokerage. We started with number two, who then moved up to the number one spot. Before coming to our seminar, she had been a close runner-up for years. The used-to-be number one probably wouldn't have given a thought to Walter Hailey and NEER Marketing if he hadn't lost his lead. But suddenly he had to know whatever it was that she found out here at Planned Marketing Associates.

Since he went through the seminar at my ranch the rivalry has been downright thrilling.

All along these two have been the runaway sales leaders at their brokerage, earning vastly more than the other brokers. Coming in second does not mean giving the house keys back to the bank, or living on pork and beans. The rivalry has, in fact, been good for them. They both make more because they're running neck-and-neck. It keeps them sharp, and makes coming to work every day a lot more fun. This shows how a friendly rivalry can be good for both the company and the rivals.

They are, indeed, friendly. They are also about as different as two human beings can be. Original Mr. Number One is an A-type hard-charger. Ms. New Number One is gentle and motherly. If she gets out of investments she could make a fortune as a cookie spokesperson, or an Ann Landers-type advice columnist.

They don't share personal styles. The other thing they don't share is trade secrets. I am honestly surprised that Ms. New Number One didn't go for a court injunction to keep Mr. Old Number One away from Canyon Springs Ranch.

Coming here was the only way he could find out what she'd learned, so she could pass him. She wasn't about to tell him. He, for his part, is not a bit more forthcoming.

Not with her.

There are other brokers, in that same office, with whom Mr. Old Number One (for all I know he's now Mr. Back On Top) is an open book. No, he's more like an open set of encyclopedias. While he hides everything from his rival, he's been telling three newcomers everything they need to know about the business. He gives them leads and shows them, in detail, what they ought to be doing.

Why does he do it?

Partly because three new kids on the block don't constitute a threat.

But mostly because they simply **asked**.

Not only did they ask, they paid attention to what he said, used it, told him how things were working out and — above all —

showed that they appreciated his help. He is a great mentor.

What you need to know about finding, and keeping, mentors is in a section of the last chapter, which is called **OPEN:**

OTHER
PEOPLE'S
EXPERIENCE
NOW!

Nobody will mind a bit if you skip ahead and read the chapter on mentors.

There are other 80/20s well worth study. Many companies put out lists of their top performers. Even if you're not in a position to ask for mentoring, you can learn a lot from the leaders just by watching what they do, and listening to offhand conversation.

Your office may have statistics about where the aggregate sales are coming from, so you can look at **everybody's** 80/20, combined. Compared against your own, this can be a valuable instrument check. Conspicuous differences between your 80/20s and company and industry norms might mean that you're missing opportunities, and need to make adjustments. Differences can, on the other hand, mean that you're onto your own lucrative sub-market. (If so, you probably want to keep it to yourself.) Comparisons often tell you both good and bad.

ACTION PLAN

80/20 To the Second Power

The Daily Action Plan you worked up at the end of the last section, based on your second 80/20, was a practice run for this exercise, which should soon cease to be an exercise and become your routine method for planning your days.

- Put your 80/20 Customer Tally Sheet, Daily Activities Log and the Daily Action Plan from the last set of exercises side-by-side.

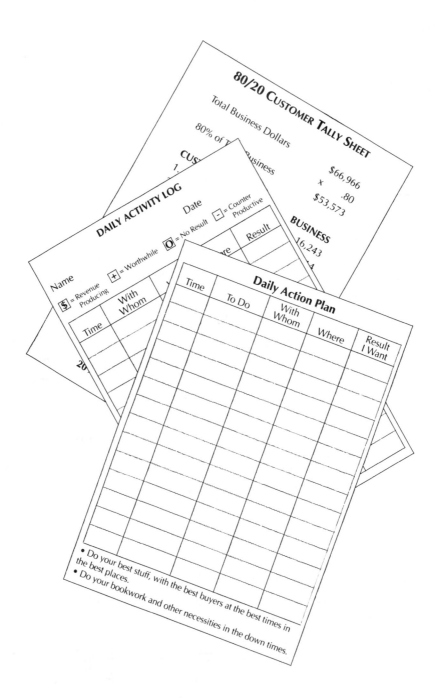

• You now have, right in front of you, in black and white, everything you need to plan the most productive working days you've ever had.

• Using the 80/20s together, work up a new and further-improved Daily Action Plan. Make sure your most powerful moments are spent with the best customers and prospects. Fill in the gaps with necessary routine tasks, paperwork and the like, and "What the Heck" calls to less promising customers and prospects.

• Carry the Action Plan in your pocket. Look at it before you go to sleep and first thing after you wake up. Follow it.

• Do what you ought to do, when you ought to do it, whether you want to or not. **NO DEBATE!**

Never Stand Still

• Don't stop looking at your 80/20s. What's true today won't be true six months from now, maybe six weeks from now. Be prepared to revise and make adjustments.

• 80/20 always gives you a goal. If you're in the top 20 percent, aim for the top 20 percent of that group, the top 4 or 5 percent overall. When you're in the top 5, go for number one seller in your company. When you're on top of your company, there will be industry leaders to challenge.

CHAPTER 3

7 to 1: The Rhythms of Your Business

YOUR OWN CENTRAL INTELLIGENCE AGENCY

Proactivity, which is the cure for much of what's wrong with American business, has been mysteriously slow to catch on. I suppose this is because proactivity takes more effort. The first step toward proactivity is getting off your hind-end. This simple move is, for many, the hardest, but it's half the game. The other half is alertness, organization and discipline. Proactivity requires, above all, **intelligence**, in every sense of the word.

Intelligence is more than IQ. All the smarts in the world won't do a thing for you until you train those brain cells to march in formation, toward a definite, doable goal.

The other side of intelligence is what the middle initial of CIA stands for. On the national level, this is everything that can be learned about foes and friends that might be used to the country's advantage. You, Ms. or Mr. Salesperson, need to be every bit as intelligence-minded as your government. You've got to establish your own personal Central Intelligence Agency. The more you know about the competitors, allies and — above all —clients and prospects, the more you can sell.

7 to 1, the title of this chapter, stands for a particularly crucial piece of intelligence about your clients and prospects. 7 to 1 is a time period, 7 A.M. to 1 P.M., which in my business was the critical selling time. If I didn't make my money in these all-important hours, I didn't make it at all.

Your 7 to 1 might be different from mine. Residential realtors are busiest in late afternoon and early evenings, because owners don't generally allow their houses to be shown at 7 a.m. If your customers run nightclubs, your best selling hours might be late afternoon and early evening, just before the clubs get busy. The best time to approach restaurateurs is the earliest moment that is **not** a peak mealtime. Financial planners tend to be freer early in the day, because they visit their clients' homes in the evenings.

The point of 7 to 1, in the NEER Marketing System, is that every customer has peak buying hours, when he or she is most receptive to your selling. To maximize your results, you've got to identify those hours and make sure that you spend them where they count — with prime customers and solid prospects. While making your calls at the right times, you should also avoid showing up at the wrong times. If you're a nuisance, there's a remote chance that somebody will say "Yes, I'll take it," to get rid of you. The overwhelming likelihood, though, is that they'll just get rid of you.

The second 80/20, which showed you what to do, and when to do it, probably revealed something about your customers' 7 to 1. If you've identified the most productive selling times, you're also looking at customers' buying times. You can't know for sure these are the **best** times, but they are, at least, acceptable. 7 to 1 takes you way beyond 80/20, though, because it takes you out of your own skin. Instead of drawing conclusions from your own daily activities, 7 to 1 requires that you study the rhythms of somebody else's business, as if it were your own. What you've got to do is to mentally live the client's day, the way he or she lives it. When you can do that, you'll know the best times for making your calls.

Walking a few miles in your clients' footwear will teach you more than 7 to 1. The better you can see things as others do, the more you can begin to unravel and solve their problems. Remember: Every problem solved is a sale made!

ACTION PLAN

Customer-watching

• Based on what you already know, rough out a daily schedule for your best client, like the example on page 80. When does the customer's workday start? End? What comes in between? Where? With whom?

• When would the customer be most comfortable having you call, and be most alert, interested and willing to buy?

_____

• Should you be making alterations in your current calling schedule? _____If the answer is yes, write out what the changes ought to be.

_____

_____

_____

CUSTOMER SCHEDULE

Customer __Charlie Boyd, Owner/Manager, Win-De-Co__

Business __Aluminum Windows__

Schedule __6:00 am to 6:30 pm__

TIME	ACTIVITY
6:00	Checks orders and deliveries
7:00	Checks rushes and special orders - opens mail
8:00	Louise, Exec Assistant, comes in
9:00	Returns calls, paperwork
10:00	Paperwork, staff meeting with manufacturing supervisors.
11:00	Tours office and plant
12:00	Lunch, job site, in office (Bubba's Bar-B-Q, Joan's Cafe)
1:00	Tours jobs, cellular #777-5950
2:00	Tours jobs, cellular #777-5950
3:00	Tours jobs, cellular #777-5950
4:00	Back in, returns calls
5:00	Sorts orders - dispatches
6:00	Tours shipping & receiving
7:00	Wednesday nites beer with the boys at Roy Dale's
8:00	Home
Evening	

Best Calling Times:

6:30 - 8:00 at loading dock, 11 am in plant.
Socialize Wed nite at Roy Dale's

• Think about some more of your top customers and how they spend their days. Are the schedules — and the best calling times — similar? _____ It may be that you'll notice a few patterns, based on professional specialties of the clients, or other common denominators:

_____

_____

_____

• With what you've learned in this exercise, you can fine-tune the Daily Action Plan you generated in the last chapter, based on your 80/20 research. The purpose is to get in sync, so you're always selling when the clients are buying.

Why Sunrise Is Prettier Than Sunset

Everybody stand now, for the first ten words of our national anthem, which happens to contain the secret of meeting and doing business with the most successful people in the world.

The anthem, as everybody remembers, starts with a question: **O say can you see, by the dawn's early light?**

The answer to the question is **Yes!** you can see, better than at any other time of day. And **Who** you can see, by the dawn's early light, are the prime influencers, shakers and movers who can do your business the most good, who you can't see easily — or at all — at any other time of the day.

Early morning is one of our most underappreciated and under-utilized resources. If you're waiting until 9:30 or 10 in the morning to start making your calls, you're throwing away a huge competitive advantage. A while back I said there are a few branches of sales that operate off-hours, because the customers live and work off-hours. For the vast majority, though, morning is the time of golden opportunity.

I sold $500 million of life insurance **before** ten o'clock. I sold it to rich folks who might not have let me through the door if I called on them **after** ten o'clock.

The rich and powerful, almost invariably, are morning people. They get up early, and are already at the office when the poor are stuck on the freeways, with a whole lot more bills at home than cash. Everybody **but** the rich spends the prime morning hours giving themselves ulcers, spilling their coffee, while they're trying to get where the rich already are — at work. And all the while the not-so-successful are wondering how come they've got so much **month** left over at the end of their **money!**

When you call Mr. Gotrocks' office at 7:00 A.M., who answers the phone? The man himself, because the support staff isn't in yet. Chances are the boss is lonely, and would love some company. Besides simple loneliness, there's a special bond between early risers that makes contacts more respectful and fruitful. Communication can really flow, because the distractions of the busy day have yet to begin.

In my early-hours calls, people were genuinely glad to have somebody to talk to. When Mr. or Ms. Rich's executive assistant came in at 8:31 A.M., I would say hello, on the way **out**, instead of trying to get by him or her on the way **in**. This was a great feeling. I literally had no competition at 7 A.M. I never did run into another life insurance salesman when I was making my early calls. When I saw my competitors, after 9 o'clock, they were cooling their heels in the lobby, waiting to see the person who just told me, "Yes, I'll take it."

Practically anyone can get an enormous jump on the competition simply by starting earlier. The magic of mornings is hardly a secret. Everybody knows Ben Franklin's "Early to bed and early to rise" and the old adage about the early bird getting the worm. But at least 90 percent of those in business ignore the common wisdom, and stay up too late, so they get up too late and get going too late.

On top of all that, an amazing number of offices make sure that **everybody** is too late, by scheduling meetings and other non-bottom-line activities at the workday's beginning. These distractions encourage pointless socializing and coffee pot seminars that eat up still more of the day's most precious minutes. By 10:30 or 11 o'clock, when people finally start making their calls, the mental edge is off, and the best time has been wasted.

Remember that in most businesses:

• 70 percent of all direct contact sales are made between 7 A.M. and 1 P.M. This is do or die time.

• 20 percent or so are made between 1 P.M. and 4 P.M. Not bad, but not enough to depend on for your living.

• 4 P.M. and on is the 10 percent zone. This is the time for office meetings, paperwork and other necessities that are **not** selling.

The accessibility of important people, who are otherwise too busy to give you a good listen (if they'll see you at all) is only part of the special importance of morning in your day. Morning makes the rest of the day happen. This is true both literally and figuratively. Your attitude is fantastic when you score some successes early. You'll carry the confidence through the day, and think more creatively. And you'll have more to do all day. When you make the early hours count, the rest of the day just takes care of itself, with follow-up on the deals you made early.

There are inner rewards, too, of rising with the sun, which have been recognized for ages by religions and philosophies. Yogis teach that transcendental meditation is particularly good early in the morning, because the world is calm, and alert peace comes to the mind more naturally. Rising with the sun is an ancient part of our Judeo-Christian tradition.

Getting started early sends an important message to yourself, that you value your time on the planet, and mean to make the most of it. When I have a sale or two under my belt by ten o'clock, I'm hard to handle — I'm a **Tiger**.

The habit of rising early is one of the advantages we farm kids have over city folk. On the farm even the second graders are up before the sun, to do their chores before the school bus comes. My dad thought if sunshine hit the milk, it would curdle.

Have you ever milked a cow? It's been years since I have, but I can remember it like I was out in the barn just this morning, the way old Little Bit would snort and try to kick over the pail, the way the milk would steam on cold mornings. It ain't easy, but when you're done there's deep satisfaction in a full milk pail. These days all our dairy products come from the store, in plastic jugs, but I still get up for milking-time, and try to fill my accomplishment-pail before breakfast, to get the most out of my day. Why not do the same? Go out to your own barn every morning and come back with a bucket full of accomplishment.

ACTION PLAN

Spring Ahead

• Adjust your mental time-keeping, the way you change the clocks every spring. Get up an hour earlier, and stay an hour ahead for the rest of the day. The results will astound you.

• If you can see your cup of coffee by daylight, you're getting up too late!

•If you're fighting rush hour traffic, you're leaving the house too late! You're also wasting time and needlessly frustrating yourself. When you're stuck in traffic, you're traveling with the sheep, following the followers. The 20 percent who earn 80 percent have passed you by.

• If getting an hour ahead of yourself works, you might want to go for 90 minutes, or even two hours.

• Dawn is for doing, not planning. This is game time. Never wait until morning to plan the day's activities. Making out the next day's Action Plan is the last thing you do at work. Carry the list home, and look at it before you go to sleep. Let your subconscious work on it all night, and you'll be hard to beat in the morning. What you seek at night, before you sleep, will seek you all night, and all the next day.

Why Eggs Are Better Than Prime Rib

Remembering milking time is bringing back all sorts of scenes of farm life back in Mesquite, Texas.

I loved to come into the house from the early morning chores. Right at the door you could smell the eggs and bacon cooking and then, in the kitchen, listen to everything spattering in the pans. Mom always made sure we always had good meals. But there was more than food served at our kitchen table. There I learned some very valuable lessons.

One morning over breakfast, Dad said to me, "Boy, set high goals and commit yourself to them. Don't just make a contribution, make a commitment." Then he grinned down at his eggs and bacon and said, "The chicken made a **contribution** to your meal, but the pig made a **commitment**." The way he made his point, I couldn't possibly miss it. I'll remember his advice as long as I remember how good Mom's breakfasts smelled and tasted.

Nutritionists will tell you that breakfast is the most important meal of the day. The successful will tell you the same thing. It is a proven fact that people are more likely to buy when they've broken bread with you. And the best bread to break is served at breakfast.

I can't remember missing a sale at breakfast. Many mornings I had three breakfast meetings with customers and prospects, back-to-back, in the same restaurant. I met the first person very early, say 6:15 A.M. This would, naturally, be a real early bird. After he or she left, I'd meet somebody at 7:30, and somebody else at 8:30. The last appointment was somebody who had already been to the office, before meeting me.

No, I did not gain 300 pounds eating 21 morning meals a week. I'd have a little something at each of the three appointments. Ordering small had at least two advantages — I didn't get fat, and I could concentrate on the other person, instead of the food. Nobody was put off that I didn't have anything but a cup of coffee and juice or fruit. No food at a lunchtime appointment might have seemed rude, but people don't worry about what you have for breakfast.

What's good about morning in general is particularly good about breakfast. People are more apt to listen and buy because there are fewer things on their minds. They haven't had time for the plant to blow up, the foreman to get mad and quit, or the customers to start yelling and complaining. Besides all that, the dollar value of breakfast is terrific. Three light breakfasts cost no more than most lunches, and they cost a whole lot less than one dinner.

The expense account mentality, and mistaken notions about what impresses people, are the only things keeping dinner meetings alive. When you try to sell at dinner, you're fighting the hour of the day, the wine, and all that gorgeous food the company is paying for. If the customer isn't distracted, he's sleepy. If the customer says "Yes," you can't count on him or her remember-ing it tomorrow. On week nights, the decision makers and sensible people would rather be at home with their families than overindulging and trying to be scintillating.

I hope this following story doesn't hurt any feelings, but it shows my feelings about dinner meetings, which I know are shared by many:

Not too long ago I flew into an Eastern city in late afternoon. The next day, bright and early, I had meetings with some of Planned Marketing Associates' most important clients. What I wanted to do, after the plane landed, was go to the hotel room, shower, order a light supper from room service and go over the next day's work. Then I'd relax and get to bed early.

But the clients — thinking they were doing me a big favor — had booked a table at their city's finest restaurant. Our reservation was late, so I had to wait in the hotel to be picked up. And there I was, at what should have been bedtime, putting down all this amazingly rich French cooking and drinking wine. I knew better than to eat and drink like that, but I didn't want to be ungracious. Even though I appreciated my hosts' generosity, I was mad — at myself and at them, for insisting I do something I didn't want to do. The food and wine kept me up all night, so by morning I was hardly at my best.

Drinks after work, in my book, fall somewhere between the Power Breakfast and the late-hours Indigestion and Insomnia Special. Breakfast, I believe, makes a better statement about you and your business. You'll never hurt your image by getting up too early for your poached eggs and coffee. Even a cocktail-lounge lizard, who rolls out of the sack at the last minute, and gets to work late, will respect you for it. That same drinker might **lose** respect for you if you match him or her drink for drink in the lounge after work. In general, the men and women who are on top of their businesses are not warming barstools at six o'clock, having two or three for the road. The successful tend to head straight home, to their families.

There are, of course, exceptions to every rule. I generally work both ends of the days, and the middle, too. Lunch can be almost as good for deal-making as breakfast.

I've always been impressed with people who don't let yesterday use up too much of today. In Fort Worth recently, the great football coach Lou Holtz said "If what you did yesterday looks like a lot, then you haven't done much today."

If there's a moral to this 7-to-1 chapter, it's this:

Live neither in the past nor the future. Let today's work absorb all of your energies and satisfy all of your strongest ambitions.

ACTION PLAN

Hailey's Good Morning Special

A fruitful breakfast meeting is no accident. This simple recipe will bring in more business with your bran muffins and coffee.

• Before you make an invitation, mentally ride the road between your prospect's home and office. The place to eat is somewhere along that route.

• Try to match the place and the person. Country types might be happiest in a down-home atmosphere, Yuppies at a place with a French name. Whatever the pick, make sure there's sufficient quiet and privacy. Go alone, and eat the food, before you make an invitation. It's especially good to be known and welcomed by the manager. If you don't know the territory, pick a reliable chain, such as Denny's.

• Keep the meeting short and to the point. Tell your invitee beforehand how much time you want to take, and don't take a minute more, unless he or she insists. If the other person wants to linger, break it off politely and go about your business.

• When one meeting is set, invite somebody else for just before, or just after. Then another. Breakfast time, which is prime deal-making time, runs from 6:30 to 8:30.

CHAPTER 4

The 15 System: When No Means Yes

HAILEY'S NEW MATH

This will be the last chapter that starts with a number, so you math phobics can relax. My numbers aren't really math, anyhow. Like the acronyms — NEER and BLT and so on — they're mostly memory aides, to streamline thought processes so you can act. The only true purpose of this book or any form of education is **action**. Food for thought, if it doesn't put food on somebody's table, does not deserve any more thought.

Fifteen is a reminder that "No" doesn't mean "No" until you have heard it 15 times. Research based on my own experience and that of my sales staffs shows that No will become **Yes** nine out of ten times — if you follow the **15 Rule**.

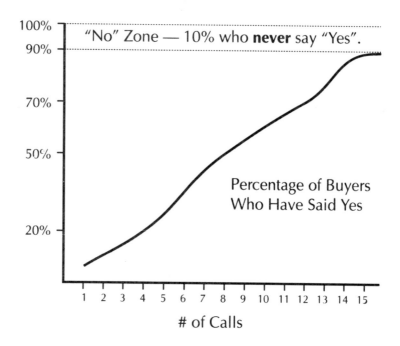

# of Calls

The 15 System

- After **4** calls, **20** percent of prospects will have bought.
- After **8** calls, **half** will have said "I'll take it."
- **12** calls, and **70** percent are sold.
- At the 15th call, **90** percent have given you a big, bright **Yes.**

The 15 System worked for me and my associates in more than 30 years of selling commodities and insurance and financial instruments to all kinds of clients, all across the country. We could bank on it. We went to the bank — often — with what it earned for us.

The 15 System, like every other component of my selling system, does not stand on its own. To make the most sense, and bring the biggest increases in productivity, it must be used with what you've learned in the previous chapters.

The **80/20s** showed **Who** your best customers and prospects are, as well as **What** kinds of contacts are most productive, and **Where** (on the phone, at lunch, etc.) those contacts work best.

- **7 to 1** is **When** you ought to be calling.
- The **15 System** is **How Many Times** you ought to call.

Taken together, 80/20, 7 to 1 and the 15 System are nothing less than a Strategic Selling Plan. Follow it, and I guarantee your persuasive performance will dramatically improve.

Only the most promising, qualified buyers — the top 20 percent, who produce 80 percent — deserve the full 15 prepared calls. Between call 1 and call 15, you can apply a sliding scale, factoring in the potential value of the new business, growing rapport with the prospect, and the hundreds of observations and feelings that grow out of repeated contacts with another human being. Naturally, buyers who can bring you the most business justify the greatest efforts. The biggest prize of all is a prime buyer who is also a prime influencer, whose decisions will be watched and followed by others. An influencer is like the Bell Cow back on the farm. Where he or she goes, the herd follows. For a Bell Cow, you want to pull out all the stops.

Another factor in deciding whether to make all 15 calls on a given buyer is your own situation. If you're swimming in qualified clients (you will be if you follow my NEER system) you can be persnickety. If you don't have many, you've got to be persistent with what you've got.

Persuasion, like every other human science, takes us beyond what can be easily expressed, into the realm of instinct and intuition. There are more things in heaven and earth, Horatio, than

Hailey can put in his marketing book (apologies to Shakespeare). Sometimes you just **know**. When you just know, you've got to be ready to do something about it.

Late one afternoon, back in my Light Crust Flour days, I was driving down U.S. 67 toward Texarkana. Selling-wise, I was in retreat. Not 10 minutes earlier Mr. Walker up in Hope, Arkansas, had told me "No" for the eighth time. The way he said it, I knew he meant it. But suddenly — Wham! — it hit me that I had to go back. So I turned around.

This was almost 5:30 P.M., way past good deal-doing time in the grocery business.

"Hi," I said.

"You just left!" If Mr. Walker was glad to see me again, he did a very good job of hiding it.

"I had to come back," I said, "I suddenly realized something. I want this account so bad..."

"I know it and I am **not** gonna..."

"Wait!" I said, "Wait a minute. If there was a way that I could ship the flour Monday and be here and go out into your stores, with your people, to help them set up displays and sell, you'd want that, wouldn't you?"

He yelled at me one more time: "Ship the son of a (expletive deleted)!"

I'll never know for sure why Mr. Walker changed his mind. It could be that I finally hit on his dominant buying motive. Or maybe he felt sorry for me. I knew, though, for reasons that I can't begin to explain, that this might be my golden moment with him.

Once in a great while, instinct and intuition have the opposite message. Every veteran persuader has run up against a **No** that is absolutely, positively, permanently carved in granite. No matter how badly you want the deal, all the inner voices are saying that you and the buyer are never going to click — and they're right.

The operative word here is **Next**! Prospects are being created faster than you can call on them. **Next** is the perfect antidote to **No**. It is one the most beautiful, healing words in the vocabulary of marketing and salesmanship. We like to have our seminar participants stand up and shout "Next!" at the top of their lungs, just to get the feel of it.

Experience shows that beyond the 15th call you're in the Land of Diminishing Returns, which is inhabited by some very nasty, weird folks. These are the No People, who get their jollies saying **No** to salesmen. They've got a club, where they brag about how many people they've turned down, and what sort of emotional damage they did. An unhappy salesperson thrills these people. I can't explain it, but I know they're out there, because I've met them. So have you, if you sell for a living. Forget about them. Let them spoil somebody else's day.

This is, however, much too early in the game to start worrying about that impossible 10 percent, because none of you have made enough calls to separate the chaff from the wheat, and bring you 90 percent success with the buyers you really want.

I'd venture to guess that practically nobody out there has gotten past calls number **3** or **4**, much less **15!**

Most salespeople — fully half of them, in my experience — quit after the first **No**. More than 80 percent have quit before the fifth call, which is just when things are starting to get good. (If you don't believe me, turn back to the 15 Rule success rate statistics.)

The quitters don't just quit, they tell everybody else in their offices that so-and-so turned them down. Everybody listens and makes mental notes, so they won't call on whoever said "No." When a new sales person comes in and says, "I'm going to call on Mr. X," they all shout him or her down, "NO, NO, NO! Bob called on Mr. X, and he won't buy." So new people don't call, either. Meanwhile, Mr. X continues to buy from the competition, mainly because no one has showed him a better way to solve his business problems. And then one day everybody looks up and sees that Mr.

X now owns half the state. He has grown, and so have his suppliers. But the timid souls who were scared away by one little No are not among them.

This sounds like a fable, but I've seen it happen, time and again.

One of our clients walked into a textbook case of a sales office with a bad case of No-itis. She had just begun selling airtime for a radio station in Louisiana, the oldest and best in her city, when she announced that she intended to call on a prospect who looked really good. The others told her, "You don't want to call on **that** guy. We've all done it. He turns **everybody** down."

They probably meant that everybody had tried him **once** — or maybe they all **thought** about calling, but changed their minds because of what office mates told them. I'll bet my ranch that not one of those naysayers got beyond the 2nd call — much less the magic 15th.

Our client, bless her, paid no attention to them. Off she marched to this big, bad prospect, who turned out to be a high school classmate, whom she had helped out in the past. He was delighted to find out that she was in town. After they finished socializing, he made a big buy of air time.

Her office mates shouted, "I can't believe it!"

You know you're onto something good when people start yelling "I can't believe it!" I've been hearing "I can't believe it!" all my life.

You'll start hearing it, too, when you stop being so afraid of **No**, and start using the 15 System.

The Two-Letter Dragon

No is the dragon business persuaders have to slay, in the quest for professional personal success.

This elemental, gut-level fear of No, does not, when you think about it, make much sense. We all feel it, though, and we run from the word as if it could kill us.

How can a two-letter, one-syllable negative have such awful power? This is one of those words that means much more than it says. It speaks to the frightened child that we all once were, and still are. We heard No! from adults long before we could talk. Beyond the childhood associations are million-year-old fears. No! sounds like being cast out by one's own kind, which for our ancestors was death. No feels like rejection and exclusion. It scares us, and hurts like crazy. An attack on the ego feels just as dangerous as the threat of bodily injury or death.

When you respond to every No at a deep emotional level, as if it really meant rejection of your entire self, selling can be misery. You're always as vulnerable as I was the night I allowed the pig farmer in East Texas to destroy my self-esteem. He didn't want to buy my insurance, and he was pretty rude about it — but nothing he did can account for the condition he put me in. "No" that night jangled every fiber of my being. I was devastated.

It is time to start pulling this two-letter dragon's teeth, and putting out its fire. We need to lose the Fear of No, once and for all.

Step One is another piece of brain programming. You want to add some new meanings of No to your mental dictionary. Then you want to check the circuitry between your ears and your brain. The object is to hear what people are saying — not what you're **afraid** they're saying.

- 9 times out of 10, **No** is **Yes** waiting, and wanting, to happen.

- This is **not** motivational happy talk. It's the truth, field-tested and proven in my own experience and that of many other successful persuaders. The 15 System, if you follow it conscientiously, will show you how true it is.

To understand what No really means, you've got to understand the reasons people don't say Yes the first time around:

- Only 1 in 10 don't buy because they don't like you or your deal.

- 9 out of 10 are not in a position to make an immediate decision. Give them time, and they'll be in position.

- Half of the non-buyers don't understand your proposal well enough to make a decision.

- The other half, even though they understand the proposal, cannot make a decision without help.

- **You** are in position to improve your buyers' understanding and provide needed decision-making help.

ACTION PLAN

Checking For Damage

When he trains in the field, Ralph Moten, our presentation and closing wizard here at Planned Marketing, has a great cure for new sellers' No-phobia. When he sees them staring off into space, working up the courage to phone a prospect, he calls them and screams something like this:

I am absolutely never, ever going to buy from you! They ought to throw you in jail, for what you're selling. Besides that, your presentation is the silliest thing I've ever heard. Your haircut's funny, too. Do not even **think** *about bothering me again — No! No! No!*

Before the shock wears off, he calls back and says, "The worst thing that can happen to you on a call just happened." Then he asks them to check for broken bones, cuts, contusions, internal damage. It didn't really hurt you, did it? he says.

His lesson hits home every time — No isn't so horrible, after all.

- You can do this exercise with a friend.

- Make a deal with him or her to call you at unexpected moments with a Prospect-from-Hades blast, like Ralph's.

• After you've had No! shouted into your ear, look yourself over for damage. There won't be any.

Money In Your Pocket

Now that you know that No won't hurt you, it's time to find how much good it's doing for you.
• Following the illustrated example on page 98, calculate the average value of each contact with a prospect you make. Simply divide your earnings in a typical week, or month, by the number of contacts you made in the same period.

_____

_____

_____

_____

_____

_____

• Now that you know what a contact is worth, whether the buyer says Yes or No, **pay** yourself — in your mind, in satisfaction and pride — for every single selling contact you make, while you're making it.

• You can have fun by thanking your next non-buyer profusely for the amount the No! was worth. When he or she asks why, explain that you earn that much every time you talk to a prospect. The buyer might be intrigued enough to reconsider and say Yes!

• Measure accomplishment in how many times you **ask**, rather than individual answers.

(A) Weekly Earnings.................$1,000.00

(B) Contacts (Phone, in-person)...........30

$$
\begin{array}{r}
33.33 \\
30\overline{)\,1{,}000}
\end{array}
$$

Divide (A) by (B)

Value to me of talking with a
prospect - buy or no buy..............$33.33

Collect my pay, every time!

The Right Kind of Persistence

Successes often come by accident, especially if you're out there where the accidents are happening. You've got to spend all the time you can in contact with clients.

There isn't a sales trainer in the world who doesn't sing hosannas about Persistence, a quality without which you absolutely cannot succeed in selling — or anything else, for that matter. Persuaders of mediocre ability who make 10 to 15 calls a day will outperform selling geniuses who only make 2 or 3. You can find exceptions, but so rarely they prove the rule and make it a **law.**

You simply can't get by (or **buy**) without persistence. But the motivators and trainers and other kinds of business gurus who talk it up are emphasizing only one kind of persistence, which, my experience has shown, is the **less important** kind. The wrong kind of persistence puts quantity of contacts over quality. If you sit somebody in front of a phone with a typed-out spiel and tell him or her to call 40 people or more a day, the law of averages will bring in a few sales, sure. But a by-the-numbers system of cold calling won't work nearly as well as building rapport and trust and mutual respect with prime clients in a series of carefully prepared and pre-heated calls.

People who teach sales can make it sound like a cross between Plane Geometry and Particle Physics. It's really as simple as people talking to people. The more you talk, the more you build bridges of mutual understanding. It's harder to sell when you're a stranger. It gets easier as you're less of stranger and more of a friend and guest — which is what you are after the fourth or fifth call.

My **NEER** system of referral and introduction, coming up **next** in this book, ensures that your first call will never be a **cold** call, because you'll always be introduced and "preheated" by someone whom the prospects knows and respects, who is one of his, or her, most influential contacts.

A few simple considerations on your part ensure that your second, fourth—or fourteenth—call is as welcome as the first. Always be:

- Brief and to-the-point.
- Pleasant and upbeat.
- **Interested** in the prospect, on all levels.

I cannot overemphasize the importance of the latter. A sincere **interest** in the client, which he or she can feel and respond to at gut level, might be the most important single factor in the sales equation.

Be Interested — Not Interesting!
If You Want To Sell — Ask Don't Tell!

These words are written in huge letters in my seminar room.(Participants shout them at the end of each class session, before I let them go for their coffee-and-bathroom breaks!)

Prospects invite you into their offices because they have a need that they hope you can fill. If you're not genuinely interested, you won't find out what that need is — much less put yourself in a position to fill it.

It is, moreover, psychologically rewarding for the prospect to spend some moments with someone who shows an interest in his or her business. Your interest alone makes you a welcome visitor.

The 15 System will not work if your **only** interest in the prospect is whether he or she is going to buy. People know when you're focused on what you can **get**, with no thought to **giving**. Remember this: As ye sow, so shall ye reap. The harvest follows the planting. This is a law. Show your sincere interest by bringing customers and prospects ideas to help their businesses, **every** time you call.

Let's listen in:

Ms. Audrey Prospect: Walter, I really appreciate you coming by. But I've got a really good agent who is serving all my needs right now. He happens to be my father-in-law. And I'm not willing to do anything that would damage that relationship right now.

Persuader: I understand. Mike, our mutual friend and your good customer, told me about your father-in-law. It makes sense to honor relationships like that. But Mike also told me that you were very progressive, and open-minded. And that it wouldn't be like you to pass up a good deal. What I'd like to do is gather some information from you, take it back to my office, and look it over to see if there's any way we could save you some money, or increase the value of your coverage. If we can do you some good, I'm sure you'd want to know about it. If you're all set, I'm sure you'd want to know that, too.

Two things might happen here:

1) Ms. Prospect might find out that her father-in-law is the world's greatest insurance agent, and the coverage plan is flawless. If so, she'll be happy to know it.

2) The far more likely outcome is that there is some way that the seller can save Ms. Prospect some money and do a better job.

Either scenario benefits the customer. Number Two could well mean a sale.

We'll listen in again:

Persuader: Hi, Myra, how was your Thanksgiving? The reason I stopped by, I've been reading so much about the health care crisis, and how that's the number-one concern nationally. I know the unions around here have been very concerned about medical insurance. Have you looked over your company's health plan lately? With your permission, I'd like to do some comparisons. I've been working with a woman at Champion Mutual who has a program to cut costs, with coverage that's actually better. The workers at the companies that have implemented it think it's great. Could I get some photocopies of your policies?

Your idea doesn't have to tie directly into your selling strategy:

Seller: Steve, I wanted to show you something I saw in *Business Week.* Here's this story about the way the game is changing in your business. They've got an item about a guy in Cleveland who has a shop just about like yours, and how he doubled his volume. Maybe you've met him.

People worry about **persistence** becoming **pestiferousness**. It doesn't, if you always drop a little on the plus side. Giving before you get opens up what we at Planned Marketing call an **Obligation Vacuum** (OV), on the buyers' side. Nature, they say, **abhors** a vacuum. The human psyche doesn't like a vacuum any more than Nature does. The more you do for someone else, the bigger the OV, and the greater the impulse, on the other person's part, to do something for you. If the other person is a potential buyer for what you're selling, a **sale** may well be what rushes in to fill the OV.

Persuaders are always too ready to be scared away by prospects' existing contacts — like Ms. Prospect's father-in-law insurance agent — as if unbreakable bonds were involved. But my experience has shown that buying/selling relationships are **always** negotiable. By offering better value my insurance company did business with men and women all over the country, many of whom had been buying from close friends and relatives all their lives.

In our seminars, we've been conducting a running survey. We ask every group if anybody has a buying relationship that he or she would **not** consider changing, if someone else offered a better all-around value.

Fewer than 2 percent have said yes!

We're talking about thousands of seminar participants a year, involved at every level in every conceivable profession and business, from brain surgery to dentistry to the law, to snack foods and construction equipment. Together they're doing hundreds of millions of dollars of business, with thousands of suppliers. And 98 percent of that business is fair game.

So don't worry about being closed out. There will always be room for you, if you have better solutions or can establish better rapport. With each call, the 15 System shows what a powerful problem-solver you are, and deepens rapport with the buyer.

On **every** visit:

• You build **Believability**, **Likability** and **Trust**, the interpersonal foundations of a sale.

• The prospect learns more and more about your product, service or idea, while you learn more about that person and the problems that need to be addressed. The more information exchanged, the closer to a sale you get.

• Your sales calls are dress rehearsals for the business relationships toward which you are working. Persistence makes a statement about how well you'll take care of prospects, when they become customers.

• And you'll always be welcomed, because you always bring something of value!

With the 15 System working for you, each call alters the basic buying decision balance, adding to the **Yes** side, while subtracting from the **No**.

In our seminars, we diagram the sales-making process as a balance. At the opening moments of your first sales call, the picture might look something like this:

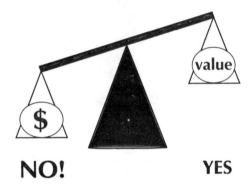

NO!   **YES**

On the left-hand side of the scale is the buyer's cost, as he or she perceives it, and on the right-hand the value of what you're offering. As long as the money counts for more in the buyer's mind, he or she is not going to say "I'll take it." The role for you, the seller, is to make value count for more than cost, and tip the balance to Yes!

On subsequent calls, if you, the seller, come by and say, "Bill, do you know such-and-such?" And he says, "How about that!" and appreciates what you tell him, the picture looks more like:

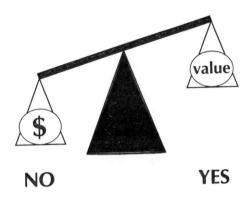

Keep calling, with valuable contributions, and the scales will, sooner or later, tip:

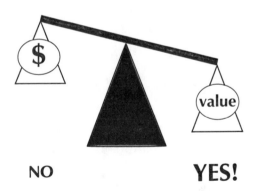

Remember that this cost-versus-value scale is extremely sensitive. The tiniest plus on value side will tip the balance and make the sale happen. You may not know what makes it happen, because the ultimate decision is made deep in the buyer's mind.

By the 15th visit — 9 out of 10 times — you and your product's value are bigger and better-looking than the customer's perception of dollar outlay.

• Remember that Value, as we showed in Chapter 1, is more than price-for-product. Value is everything about what you're selling that benefits the buyer — especially **you**.

ACTION PLAN

Exit/Entrance Lines

Compared to the others, this chapter is a little skinny on Action Plans. That's because the 15 System **is** an Action Plan, self-explanatory and ready to use. If you've read this far, you know enough to start using it, making multiple prepared calls on your best prospects.

• Each time you call, **add** a little value. Take an idea that will help your prospect grow his or her business. Look for such ideas in:

> • Newspapers
> • Trade journals
> • Other businesses like your clients'

• Ask your mentors and office mates for business-building ideas.

• Look everywhere for such ideas. The more you look, the more you'll find!

• Pass on any sort of information that the buyers can use.

• Give your client somebody to call on. Make a referral, with a hearty endorsement, to a likely candidate for the client's product or service.

• Congratulate the client on recent business or personal triumphs.

• Ask for business or personal advice. This might sound odd, but an appeal for a bit of help is one of the most endearing things you can do.

• And always use an **exit** line that's also an **entrance** line, so you leave with an invitation to come back. It'll go something like this:

Seller: I can see that you're not quite ready. I'll call again in 60 days or so (or whatever the appropriate time period) to bring you up to date on new product developments.

• **Do not** use your exit/entrance lines until you have **asked** your prospect if he or she is ready to buy yet! The buyer may well be waiting for **you** to make it happen. Believe it or not, 64 percent of sales calls end without anyone asking for an order.

• If your own words fail you, try one of our favorite closing lines:

Seller: Do you see any good business reason why we shouldn't start this now?

Solving The Whole Problem

It's time to do a little more mental programming.

A while ago we rewrote the definition of **No**, and fixed your ear circuits, so **No** sounds less discouraging and more like a **Yes** waiting to happen — which, in fact, it is, when you use the 15 System.

Now we're going to get rid of a word altogether, just disconnect it and throw it away. The word is **Failure**.

There are no **Failures** — there are only **Results or Outcomes**. How good these outcomes are, is entirely up to you. When you're thinking correctly, there is no such thing as a sales call failure — whether or not the customer says "Yes, I'll take it." Every call, whether or not you get a sale, is a **Research Call**, and every call is a **Success**.

Research yields knowledge, which is power in the buyer-seller relationship. The more you know about a buyer and his world, the more he perceives you as an expert in your field and trusts your judgment. This works, every time.

Now I'm going to sound like one of those Sixties Flower Children: Our 15 System is all about Mind Expansion. Your outlook expands, and you observe the world differently, so there's less negativity and fewer barriers between you and where you want to be. Meanwhile, you're observing **more** of the world. Absolutely everything that you see/hear/feel on a sales call can be grist for the selling mill.

First you must see the business problems that your product, service or idea can solve.

Ask yourself this question: What's the best outcome this person could hope for, from buying what I'm selling? Then go to work to make sure that it happens.

When the narrower business problems have been addressed, expand your perception to **all** of the client's problems, and what you can contribute to their solutions. Keep prospects talking, and their real desires and fears will surface. The more they talk, while you listen totally, the more the focus is taken off your persuasive role, so resistance to you diminishes.

From the beginning, I had a sign in my office that read, **We Are The Fastest-Growing Insurance Company In America Because We Recognize People's TOTAL PROBLEMS, And Help Solve Them.**

People always misunderstood the sign. They'd say, "Oh yeah, you help handle their total insurance problems." Wrong. I meant problems in life, in the world. On calls I'd listen until I found out what kind of big problems people had. If somebody said, "I've got a kid I can't straighten out," I'd call a psychologist friend of mine, who once worked with my own family. If somebody was worried about any problem, I'd search out information, and the name of somebody who could help.

• You can have everything you want in life, if you help others solve their **total problems.**

Liking and interest can be faked, but not for long. Behind these persuasive techniques must be sincere mutual regard. The best persuaders make friends out of their customers. Friendship cements the working relationship — and it makes working immeasurably more rewarding. The friendships I made, selling flour, then insurance, might have started with business, but they outlasted the business by decades. I've been a pallbearer for several old, dear friends whom I first met on sales calls.

Winning Style

Back in the Great Depression, we kids rarely had the luxury of wearing new clothes. Since I didn't have an older brother, my hand-me-downs came from the son of one of my mother's best friends, Eula Humphreys. The fit would have been perfect if I had been about 6 inches taller, and 50 pounds heavier. Cut short by my mother, and hitched up with a belt, those big old pants looked ridiculous. Mother would tell me not to worry, because I'd grow into them. She was wrong. My waistline isn't big enough for those pants yet.

One day when I was feeling particularly mopey about my clothes, Mother said to me, "Of all the things you wear, your expression is the most important." This time she was right. The lesson stuck — it still sticks. What was true for that farm boy is still true for me today. And it's true for everybody, particularly those you persuade others to say Yes! to make a living.

If you want people to tell you Yes, you've got to give them a Yes first. A big, bright smile is **Yes!** written across your face. Valuable information isn't enough to take to your clients and prospects. You want to make everybody's day a little bit brighter, just because you visited or phoned. Give freely of the nine Positive Power Gifts,

which were spelled out by M. R. Kopmeyer:
- Gift #1: Make others feel **ACCEPTED!**
- Gift #2: Make others feel **APPROVED!**
- Gift #3: Make others feel **ADMIRED!**
- Gift #4: Make others feel **APPRECIATED!**
- Gift #5: Make others feel **IMPORTANT!**
- Gift #6: Be **AGREEABLE...agree!**
- Gift #7: Give others the **ATTENTION** they crave!
- Gift #8: Make others feel **NEEDED!**
- Gift #9: Fill the **NEED FOR OUTSIDE HELP!**

Of course the outer person can't be ignored. In dressing for success, there are no across-the-board rules. The idea is to dress in a mode familiar to your buyer, one status-level above her or him. The ideal perception on the seller's part is a combination of comfort and respect. When I had agents who officed in big grocery warehouses, brokering insurance and savings programs to the grocers who were at the warehouse buying stock for their stores, I asked my employees to dress like the warehouse sales personnel, with sweaters and name tags.

No matter where you're working, it never pays to be conspicuous or flashy. Silk suits and a lot of gold jewelry gives the wrong message to a buyer — it says you're making too much money from his or her purchases. When you don't know how your contacts are going to look, low-key classic conservatism is the best bet, for both men and women. Clothes and accessories should never distract from you and the business at hand. Shakespeare says it best:

Costly thy habit as thy purse can buy,
But not oft expressed in fancy; rich, not gaudy,
For the apparel oft proclaims the man

You'll notice that Shakespeare didn't say anything about flip charts, audio-visuals and all the other props and doo-dads that a Nineties seller can haul to a presentation. He was, as usual, showing wisdom. A little bit of selling apparatus goes a long way.

Sometimes salespeople try to hide behind their printed-matter and other "aids" out of shyness. This is a self-defeating exercise. You want as little as possible between you and the prospect.

One thing Shakespeare would have mentioned, if such a thing had existed back then, is a good wristwatch. Don't look at your watch too often — this is rudeness — but never forget it's there, ticking away valuable seconds and hours. Without being abrupt, you should use as little time as possible on calls. In our *Anatomy Of A Perfect Sale*, which this book does not cover, we teach that an ideal sales presentation runs no longer than 7 minutes. Your call should run longer than 7 minutes only if the buyer asks, explicitly, for more of your time.

When you are romancing the super successful — everyone's ideal clientele — you should never, ever waste their time. Too many people believe that they're so charming and entertaining that anyone would want to spend all day with them. Don't wait until others have had enough of you. Leave a little bit before they want you to leave, and they'll follow you out to your car!

Even when the buyer does want to spend all day with you, be on your way as soon as your business, with a few friendly words, is finished. If you act as if your time is valuable, others will assume it is, and appreciate it accordingly. The impression that you're in demand builds your value, in others' eyes. I taught my employees, and now my seminar participants, never to kill time during business hours, where business contacts may see you. Spend your downtime at home, after work and on weekends. Walk in a hurry, even if you're on the way to the bathroom. Never drop in on a contact just to be dropping in.

Always be on purpose! Others will respect you for it.

❖ ❖ ❖

PART TWO

FROM FEAR TO NEER

5

Marketing for the 21st Century

A PLACE TO THINK

How many of you have your own perfect thinking place, where mind, body and soul vibrate in harmony, like a church organ sounding a chord? An undisturbed hour in such a place can be as refreshing as a week at the seashore — and as educational as a semester of night school. Where the air and electricity are just right, new ideas and insights come by the dozen. Your place might be a park bench, cafe table, a beach or a stump you like to sit on in your own back yard. No matter who holds title, it is all yours, spiritually speaking, whenever you need it to be yours.

If you don't have such a place, please find one. Consider this an assignment. No, consider it a course requirement.

Once you've found your place, I want you to go there and tune out worries and pressures, and give yourself the benefit of your own best counsel and thoughts. Chances are good that the ideas you need are already in your head, waiting — and wanting — to come to the fore. Go back to your thinking place whenever you feel the need.

Sometimes we must retreat to advance.

My own thinking spot happens to be on the porch of the main house here at Canyon Springs Ranch, which overlooks the valley of the Guadalupe River. Something about the view of the river and the hills beyond inspires me to see clearly and deeply into myself. The ideas flow just like the spring-fed, cool Guadalupe. I don't know why the place works so well for me, but it does.

I can't help but notice that it works for other people, too. The thousands of people who come to our seminars every year are drawn to the porch and my spot. I don't mind at all if they borrow it, as long as they give it back.

This opportunity to get away from familiar surroundings and do some fresh, creative, constructive thinking is one of the more valuable aspects of the Power of Persuasion experience. It may, indeed, be the second-best thing about the seminars. The first is NEER, the system at the core of our teaching.

A philosophical sort of atmosphere, which we have here at the ranch, is just right for teaching NEER, which is really a philosophy of person-to-person communication. My young associate Steve Anderson calls it a way of life. Some folks, though, can't see beyond the powerful marketing system that NEER is. The unique perceptions of NEER are always exciting. Everybody, it seems, gets something different out of it, and they're always charged-up about what they get. Sometimes their new insights expand our own understandings.

Very early in our last session, the perceptual lightning struck

Sanders Thompson, a commercial real estate broker. "This," he proclaimed, "is **the** marketing system for the 21st Century!" The old systems, he said, are dead, or so close that somebody ought to put them out of their misery. We've been saying this all along, but it was great to share this Sanders' mighty "Aha!" and hear him work up what were — to him — new ideas.

There have, indeed, been enormous changes in American business conditions since World War II. Once upon a time there was more money chasing fewer goods, and you could sell simply by putting something reasonably attractive where the consumers could get at it. Advertising was usually enough to get them moving in your direction. The Law of Averages would bring you what the ads didn't — call on enough people and you'd hear "Yes, I'll take it!" often enough to make a living. This was the Golden Age of Cold Calling, of Smilin' And Dialin'. Sales trainers emphasized quantity of contacts over quality, and sheer numbers of calls over preparation. Trainers told sellers to make 5 or 10 or 15 calls a day (the numbers varied) and success would, inevitably, come.

Unfortunately, many are still hearing yesterday's wisdom. The **Law of Averages** — which brings you the occasional Yes! — might have been good enough 30 years ago, but these days it is a formula for disappointment, or worse. The **Law of Leverages**, which NEER relies on, gets you farther, faster.

Much of the change we face has been economic, and a direct result of America's entry into the Global Marketplace — an entry we don't seem to have been prepared for, either economically or emotionally. For years the **Re-Active Managers** (remember **RAMs?**) had the continent all to themselves, and operated under a sort of gentleman's agreement that nobody who wears a suit and tie should have to work too hard, or — especially — **think** too hard. Suddenly, though, here came these gate crashers from the other side of the Pacific. I call them **HEAT** people. **H**ungry **E**ager **A**ssertive **T**igers. We all know what happens when Tigers walk into a roomful of sheep.

Lunch happens.

Persuasion must be suited to its times. NEER, a proactive system for **seeking** out the most qualified prospects, and preparing them to **see** you in the best possible light and **hear** you with the greatest respect and receptiveness, is the system for the present and future.

If you keep on doin' what you've been doin' — what makes you think you're not gonna keep on gettin' what you've been gettin'?

More than economics have changed since the Smilin' and Dialin' Days. New technologies have made it harder to reach people, if they don't want to be reached. The situation is ironic, because many of the devices — FAX machines, voice mail, electronic mail, and so on — are supposed to enhance communication. What they really do is give people new ways to hide. This is Stealth Technology, so the buyers can disappear, just like electronically cloaked fighters and bombers. If you can't find 'em, you sure can't sell 'em.

Attitudes have changed, too. The public is increasingly irritated with cold-call telemarketing, which many companies still rely on. Cold phone contacts may well be outlawed, because of growing consumer pressure for regulatory legislation.

NEER will never be illegal, because the NEER calls are never cold. And the buyers won't ever be STEALTH-y, because they've heard about you from someone important to them. They have been pre-heated.

Once you understand it and use it, NEER will put you in front of more qualified, less resistant buyers on a regular basis. It will also predispose them to say Yes! to your product, your service or your idea. NEER won't get you what you want from every single contact — nothing will — but it will bring you more success than you've known, probably more than you thought possible. At the same time it saves you the trials and tribulations of trying to do business with absolute strangers who couldn't care less about what you're trying to tell them about, or **you.**

NEER gives the lie to that wisdom about physical fitness —with this system you can **gain** without **pain.** Whatever your business is, your results-per-effort ratio will go up. After I put the system to work for me in selling, my closing ratio went from 1 sale in 10 calls to 8 in 10. NEER can be used to win a promotion, find a job, improve your social standing, raise money for charity, meet the powerful and influential, teach more effectively, improve your grades in school. You can even have better relationships with family and friends. Of all the thousands of our seminar participants, **not one** has been unable to apply NEER to his or her professional situation!

This isn't to say we don't come up against some doubt. A certain amount of doubt and resistance is a normal response to NEER, or any other new concept — it may, indeed, be the healthiest response. I don't mind at all when somebody stands up and says, "I can see how NEER helped you sell business and personal insurance to retailers through their wholesalers, and how it could work for people selling the same sort of products, in a similar deal. But how in the world can it help **me**?"

When people talk like this, they're thinking, and they're ready to think some more. They are opening up.

One of our more profound doubters was the president of a company that sells huge, extremely expensive, industrial equipment — an absolutely non-universal product with an atypical, tiny clientele. He liked the idea of NEER, he said, but it wasn't going to do him a bit of good.

I love this sort of challenge!

We had a little skull session with him at the seminar, and came up with a workable NEER plan, which we then challenged him to try. He took the challenge and the next time he called he was telling us about his new business successes.

NEER, when you give it a fair try, will run doubt right out of town and starve fear to death. It works for universal products sold to John and Jane Doe, and specialized goods and services for the tiniest niche markets. It has worked too often, for too many people, for you to imagine that the NEER system is on trial. **You** and your ability to **understand** and **believe in** and **adapt** and **use** the system — this is what's on trial. I'm asking you to give it a fair trial, before you deliberate and reach a verdict.

Between now and then, I'm also asking you to tolerate a little bit of initial confusion. It won't be much, and it won't be for very long. NEER concepts and processes are more psychological, and a bit more subtle and complex than what we've covered so far. I'll give you NEER the way we present it in seminars — in pieces, with exercises to walk through the principles, to see how they work, and walk-around looks at the whole system, from different angles, up close and from a distance. Now and again I'll lecture a little. Since NEER is a 360-degree system, which must be **understood** to be **used**, and **used** to be **understood**, you must learn it in 360 degrees. Read my words, do the exercises and look at the graphics, but pay closest attention to the concepts behind the ink on these pages. Somewhere there's a place for you to take hold of NEER. Once you've got hold of it, you can pick it up and **use** it.

6

NEER™ 101: Basic Theory

LESSONS OF THE DONNER PARTY

What's true in one area of human life is usually true in another. An article in a science magazine shows that one of the basic principles of NEER was working back in 1846, high in the Sierra Nevadas. The article is about the Donner Party, a group of pioneers who got snowbound in the mountains, where almost half of them died.

What, at this late date, can be learned from a 150-year-old disaster?

Quite a bit, if you analyze the old events in new ways, as an anthropologist at the University of Washington did. He found an unmistakable pattern — which illustrates a universal lesson – in who lived and who died in the Donner Party. Members of family groups were much more likely to survive than those who were traveling alone. Virtually none of the loners lived, even though they were mostly young bachelors, who should have been tougher than children and middle-aged parents and aunts and uncles. Affiliation with a group turned out to be more important, in this test of survival, than mere muscle.

There is **power** in human-to-human contact. Interpersonal ties are life-promoting even when there is no threat to survival. Married people live longer, as do those with any sort of social connections. Whatever their age, gender or health, socially isolated people have death rates **twice** that of the those with family ties, friendships or group memberships.

The lessons of the Donner Party apply, in spades, to business. Careers die for the same reason as those poor bachelor pioneers. The biggest reason people fail in business is that they don't make enough contacts with other people. They remain unconnected, either because they don't recognize the value of connections, or because they're scared to make them. My experience shows that the second reason is more prevalent. People are afraid to reach out to others, to form business relationships that are also **friendships** and **strategic alliances**, because they're afraid others will turn them down. They won't ask for anything because they're terrified of No, and absolutely sure they're going to hear it.

Persuaders who are afraid of the interpersonal try to overcompensate by memorizing product features, specifications, performance parameters. They spend enormous amounts of time rehearsing presentations, with flip charts, slides, videos and all the other doodads that marketing departments love to put out.

This is sad, because if they don't have people skills, they won't have anybody to **show** it to, or **tell** it to, or — especially— **sell** it to. It's sadder still, because isolation means loneliness, and sadness.

As my dad said, the intelligent know **everything,** the wise and the rich know **everybody.** He might have added that the happy know everybody, too.

Knowing everybody, and knowing them the right way, is what NEER is all about. NEER is about the impression you make **before** the first impression. With this system people will think of you favorably and respect you before the first face-to-face, because of what they've heard about you from others.

It is time, once and for all, to quit believing in the Self-Made Man and Self-Made Woman. There are no such people, only a myth. Many have, indeed, overcome poverty and other enormous obstacles to achieve success. But nobody did it alone. All success depends on goodwill, cooperation and assistance. It depends, too, on the examples others have set.

You cannot make it alone! If you've been trying to, it's time to come in out of the cold.

The higher you rise, the more you depend on others, and the more they depend on you. Trying to deny interdependency, and trying to do without it, is a virtual guarantee that you won't rise very far, and that, whatever your job title and net worth, you'll **feel** like a failure.

One of the Japanese competitive edges has been keiretsu, a system and a spirit of close cooperation, which recognizes the interconnectedness and mutual obligations of those who do business together. In an island nation, poor in resources, the Japanese long ago formed the habit of banding together, first for survival, then for mutual enrichment. We could use a little more of this sort of cooperative spirit, on all levels, individual, corporate, community and national. NEER is keiretsu's American cousin. With it the networks of buyers and suppliers with whom you have contact become **strategic alliances,** working to build everybody's business.

The days of the adversary relationship of vendors and suppliers is passing. A new value-added, two-way method has changed marketing — permanently, in my opinion, and for the better. The win-win business philosophy has always worked, but now it's being talked about.

When you keep your eyes and mind open, you can see life's universal lessons confirmed wherever you look. On a hill not far from here, there's a house going up. The workers just finished clearing and grading the lot, and now the trucks are hauling in stone and crushed rock for the foundation. As they go about their work, I've been thinking of the importance of foundation building in our lives. From a very young age, we start building a base of goodwill, connections and a reputation with other people. We go on building, adding to and strengthening our contacts. The future will stand on the interpersonal foundation we're working on right now. Without a solid base, your career will be like the biblical house built on sand. When the winds blow, and the rain falls, it will not stand.

What A Difference An E Makes

My acronyms, like the numbers and pretend-mathematical formulas, are meant to make concepts easier to remember, and easier to **use**. If you stick on big, simple labels, you can grab what you need off the mental shelves in a hurry.

We say **NEER** instead of **N**aturally **E**xisting **E**conomic **R**elationships for exactly the same reason the big letters on the front of the soup can say Cream of Mushroom instead of "Water, Mushrooms, Modified Food Starch, Cream, Corn Starch," and so on. When you're fixing lunch, you need to know the flavor, not all the ingredients.

I was using NEER, and selling the concept to partners and corporate participants, before I knew what to call it.

The biggest success with NEER, which made me and my partners lifetime fortunes, was the system to sell business and personal insurance to grocers through their wholesalers. We put in the deal first at the Affiliated Foods warehouse in Dallas. Besides giving us a start, Affiliated brought me into contact with David Keener, then the wholesalers' general manager, who became the most important business relationship in my life. Eventually David left Affiliated and joined our venture, which owed a great deal of its subsequent success to him. David and I were, and are, the original business odd couple. He's as quiet and analytical as I am outgoing and impulsive. The combination was, and is, powerful for both of us, because we each have what the other **needs**.

From Affiliated, we expanded our insurance system to other warehouses nationwide, and then began insuring the wholesalers' suppliers as well as customers. All we did, really, was to launch our insurance boat onto a multi-billion dollar river of business that had been flowing for a long time. Looking back, it seems surprising that nobody thought of it before. But the idea was revolutionary. It caught on so big that we were very quickly able to buy the company that was providing most of our policies.

Like most revolutionary ideas, this one met with a lot of resistance. And at first I had some trouble expressing what, exactly, made it work so beautifully.

One day I was drawing out our whole grower-to-grocer system for Tom Friedberg, an executive at CNA Insurance up in Chicago. You could see the light bulb come on over Tom's head. "That is a **N**aturally **E**xisting **R**elationship — I like that idea! This is a great way to market," he said. I came out of the meeting with a package policy for our customers from CNA. This is not to mention a new friendship with Tom, one of the greatest brains in insurance. Tom's most recent victory has been to bring Ranger Insurance from also-ran to industry leader.

I used **NER** to explain our concept until another meeting in New York City, when I was showing our deal to some heavy hitters on Wall Street. Among them was Gus Levy, chairman of Goldman,

Sachs, who had just taken our company public. I drew my grower-to-grocer picture, and talked about the NER system we were part of. But Gus stopped me.

"No," he said, "You don't have just N-E-R. You've got a Naturally Existing **Economic** Relationship."

After Gus spoke up, I could see the idea catching on with all those brokers, some of whom had been very skeptical. The people around the table talked about why **Economic** was so important in the dynamics of our system. I've been talking about **NEER** ever since. It makes it easier for both the listeners and me to understand what I'm talking about and remember it and, most important, apply it.

Gus was absolutely right about the significance of **Economic** relationships in our company back then. The extra **E** is just as important today. It is, in fact, the keystone of our concepts and system.

Take away the **E** and **NEER** becomes **NER**, and 80 percent of the power is gone.

We all know what a **N**aturally **E**xisting **R**elationship is. It's anybody you know, for any reason: friends, neighbors, relatives, people at church, sorority sisters, Army buddies, members of clubs you belong to, college alums and high school classmates. Life, at some time or another, threw you together, and you still remember each other's names — this is the baseline NER. At the high end, NERs can be very important people to you, for reasons of affection, kinship, or group affiliation.

The **NER** relationship is the basis of **referral selling**, which is where most beginners start. After neophytes get their product training and presentation kits, the bosses point them to everybody, and anybody, they know. "Plan your work, and work your friends," is the formula, particularly in insurance and other universal financial products and services.

Aggressive, "sic 'em" tactics, which unscrupulous companies

encourage, have given referral selling a bad name. But there's really nothing wrong with it — a NER relationship is better than no relationship at all. When I was starting out, I tried to sell insurance policies to my family and friends, just like every other green agent. (If you haven't made your friends **before** you go into insurance, it's too late!)

There may be nothing terribly **wrong** with referral selling, but there isn't anything particularly **right** about it, either. For making business-related contacts, family or social connections are a relatively weak foundation. Much better results can be had by learning your business and building a record of success **before** you call on friends and relations. Wait until they've heard about how well you're doing, before you call, and your chances of hearing Yes! skyrocket, while the strain on your relationships plummets.

Most of us can count on at least a respectful hearing from friends and relatives, and maybe an occasional sale. Still, though, there is no basic, compelling reason — beyond personal obligations — for social contacts to consider doing business with you.

But now I want you to think about what happens when Mr. or Ms. Important comes back from lunch at the Rich and Powerful Club and listens to the messages on voice mail. Some are personal calls, some business. Some of the business calls are suppliers and other work-related contacts and some are customers.

Who gets called back first, and heard most attentively?

• The customers.

Why?

• Because they're the people who provide the money that keeps ImportantCorp in business.

Who gets called next?

• Other business-related contacts.

Why?

• In the business world, business — selling, buying or otherwise — comes before the purely personal.

There are, of course, exceptions. Family emergencies might put calling home at the top of the list. Romantic types might want to squeeze in a quick "I love you" call. But, in normal circumstances, the most serious attention will be given to business matters.

We're talking about **NEER**'s second **E**. In the context of business — and your persuasive work is business — the most powerful relationships are economic. Upon this rock the NEER system is founded.

Let's do some more make-believe:

Pretend now that one of your better customers calls you or sends a note. The message is that he or she has been buying something-or-other from Sam Seller, and the relationship has been a great boon. Sam is reliable and honest, his line of something-or-other is very good, with a fair price. You might want to know about it, too.

After you get this message, Sam calls and says he has something that he'd like to tell you about. It will take only seven minutes to find out if it might be of value of you. When, he wants to know, would it be convenient to see you?

Will you refuse to see him? I doubt it very much, because he came to you on the shoulders of a valuable business relationship. Dismissing Sam or treating him rudely might say the wrong thing about how much you care about your customer. Even if you're perfectly happy with your current brand of something-or-other, and old friends with the salesperson, you'll give Sam a listen, because of who told you about him.

A listen is hardly a sale — but it's a start. In this case it's probably a lot better than what you would have given Sam Seller if he'd come to you out of the blue.

Remember this:

　　• A persuader who comes to a buyer in the established stream of business relationships will get a better hearing than someone operating out of that stream.

• The persuader will get an even better hearing if she or he comes with a good word from a valued customer. Why? Because customers are where the money is!

• People look sharpest, and listen closest, to where their money is coming from. As my dad used to say, the human mind will "foller the dollar."

This is **Fundamental NEER**, in action.

When you turn it around, and look at it from your own point of view — that of the seller — it is clear that an ideal approach to a prospect is through one of his or her valued customers. The chances of being turned away are zero, or pretty close to it.

• Make your first approach from the high ground, where the money is coming from!

The Atomic Theory of Business

Scientists tell us that the best theories are those that explain the most complicated things in the simplest way. A theory lives until somebody comes up with a better one, which explains more with greater simplicity. For centuries people tried to understand chemistry in terms of the four elements, Earth, Air, Fire and Water. But then somebody decided that things are really made of fundamental particles. Chemical elements break down into atoms, which can joint venture with other atoms to form molecules. Atoms and molecules explain a whole lot more than Earth, Air, Fire and Water. Nowadays we know that atoms have their own fundamental particles, but the basic theory is still a keeper.

NEER is the atomic theory of business relationships and human influence.

What you, the business person, need to understand is the whole crazy universe of people's transactions with other people. You need to predict, and do, whatever will encourage the best of them to do their best transactions with you. Everything, in the world of business, is owned or controlled by a human being. To get what we need we must deal with other people, every day. Most people see all this as chaos. They find their way through it haphazardly, without training, hoping and praying that something good will come their way, unable to adequately explain either successes or failures.

NEER brings order out of chaos, along with a much greater measure of predictability and control. It works according to a few, easily understood Natural Laws. It also breaks things down to fundamental units, just like the atomic theory.

The fundamental unit of NEER is two people, one buying and one selling. We'll call it an **N**, to avoid confusing it with big NEERs, which are systems. An **N** is a:

• **N**aturally. Because the exchange, whatever it is, is appropriate and mutually beneficial. It is a flow, as natural as water running downhill.

• **E**xisting. Ongoing, and not a one-time deal.

• **E**conomic. Of course, because one is buying and one selling.

• **R**elationship. The ongoing exchange means there is a relationship. The **trust** implicit in an established relationship is critical. Without trust, you don't have a NEER.

Of course there's no such thing as a single **N**, all by itself. The person buying from A will be buying other things from B and C, but selling stuff manufactured from A, B and C's products to D and F, who might be buying still something else from A's subsidiary G. And on and on.

These little **N**s are, in this respect, like highly reactive atoms, which are always trying to hook up with something else. The system of economic relationships to which you belong — whoever you are — would, if you drew the whole business out, reach from here to Waxahachie, and make the DNA molecule look simple.

It doesn't pay to follow these chains of Ns to their bitter ends. You, the seller, gain very little by knowing who makes the high explosives used by the miners who dug up the diamonds that your best customer's biggest supplier gave to his wife.

It might, on the other hand, do you a great deal of good to know who your best customer's biggest supplier is, and what he or she supplies, and whether the supplier might be able to use the product, service or idea you represent. 80/20 will tell you how good a prospect this supplier might be. Then you might want to start looking at the supplier's suppliers and customers.

The NEER systems that count are easy-to-recognize **flows** — goods, services and ideas flowing one way, money the other. On a diagram of all the **N**s involved, they'd look like creeks and rivers on a map. These are what you want to find, and follow.

The one that my partners and I followed, until K-Mart bought our company for $78 million, was Grower-To-Grocer. Here was this long-established chain of business relationships, all the way from the farmers to the families buying peas, carrots and cornflakes. We didn't sell insurance to the consumers, but they benefitted from our arrangement, because the sellers and buyers up the line saved money. **All** costs in an economic chain are ultimately borne by the consumer. All savings can benefit the consumer. If they don't, they ought to.

Theoretically speaking, an **N** is an **N** is an **N**. Somebody's selling and somebody else is buying. Practically speaking, which side you're on can make a big difference. When you're riding in on a good word from one of the people in the N, it makes a huge difference which side you're coming from!

We call the relationship when you're on the **buying side** N_1. On the **selling side** it's an N_2.

Grower to Grocer

NATURALLY EXISTING ECONOMIC RELATIONSHIPS

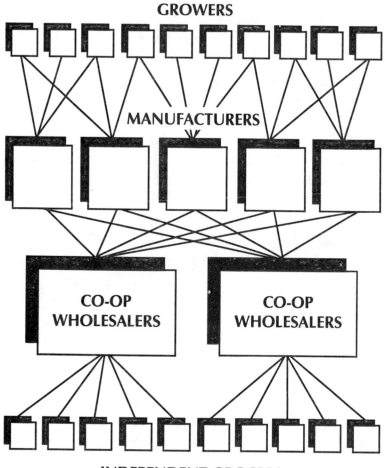

This distinction between **buyer's side** and **seller's side** is every bit as important, in your persuasive business, as learning **left** from **right** is for kids. **Where** you are, in each of your business and economic relationships, is **who** you are, in the eyes of your business contacts. And **who** you are governs what you can comfortably **ask for** and **expect** from those contacts.

Think about the N_1s and N_2s in your own business. Categorize your contacts: Who's an N_1? Who's an N_2? Recognizing this all-important distinction — and governing your actions according to it — must become automatic. This is something you must **know**, right up front.

Trying to do NEER business without a firm grasp of N_1 and N_2 is like trying to have a good social life without knowing **male** from **female**. If you can't tell the difference, you're going to have all sorts of embarrassments and frustrations.

When you're sure you've got the distinction down, ask yourself this: Is your **influence**, and the **risk** you feel when you try to use your influence, greater or lesser in an N_1 or N_2?

- We'll look at the N_1 first, where you're the buyer.

N_1 Buying Side

Instant **influence** is greater
perceived risk is small

Influence flows most smoothly and easily in the direction of the **money.** If you're holding the wallet, you can ask the other person to lend an ear for a few minutes, with every confidence you'll be heard. You can ask without the feeling that you're putting yourself at **risk**.

- Now let's look at the other situation, where you're selling.

N$_2$ Selling Side

Instant influence is less
perceived risk is greater

The dynamic here is entirely different. When you're dealing with customers, your automatic influence is less, and the feeling of risk greater.

A few pages back we showed the power of the N$_1$ in action, when the customer told you about a salesman and his product. Then the salesman called and asked if you had a few minutes to hear about his product.

What did you say?

- Yes.

Why did you say it?

- Because he was coming to you from the **buying side**, where **your money** comes from.

And why was the customer comfortable telling you about this salesman and his product?

- Because the dynamics of your NEER relationship gives him or her more automatic **influence** and less **risk**.

But try to imagine the reverse situation, where one of your suppliers calls you, the customer, to tell you about a salesman and his product. This is harder to picture, isn't it? Why?

- Because the flow here isn't as comfortable. It is, indeed, very possible that your supplier wouldn't tell you about the salesman and his product, because he or she wouldn't feel **comfortable** doing it. Approaching you, the customer, might feel more **risky.**

All things being equal, this is how the real world works. You can count on more automatic influence, and a lesser feeling of risk, when you approach prospects with referrals from their customers. This is an easy, powerful way to say "Hello."

Of course business goes way beyond first meetings, and NEER goes way beyond the customer-to-supplier N_1 relationship. In this respect our two kinds of NEER relationships, N_1 and N_2, are like the two kinds of nuclear power, fission and fusion. When mankind developed nuclear bombs and power, fission came first, because A-Bombs and fission reactors are easier to understand and engineer. Once we got the hang of that, we tried an H-Bomb, unleashing the fusion reaction, immensely more powerful than fission. The fusion reactor, which may solve the world's energy problems for all time, is still in the works, though, because fusion is trickier to harness and control.

The N_1 relationship, like fission, comes first. Here you enter NEER. N_2, which relies on the immense power of established buyer-to-seller relationships, is your future. In this case, though, the future can be grasped. N_2 systems are sustainable, and controllable, and proven in service. Planned Marketing Associates, in this respect, is at least 50 years ahead of the physicists and engineers.

My own highest-earning NEER was N_2, supplier-to-buyer, selling insurance to the grocery wholesalers' customers, through the wholesalers. From the individual grocer's point of view, the system worked because of the longstanding, trusting relationship with the wholesale warehouse. We became part of a familiar, comfortable, regular buying cycle, to the point that our insurance premiums appeared on the wholesalers' monthly bills. We eliminated all the surprises, which might have created resistance on the grocers' part. All of this made it easier, and more natural for the grocer to say Yes! Beyond that, our NEER system enabled us to become a **Buyer For**, rather than **Seller To** our customers. Economies of scale enabled us to cut costs enormously and tailor coverage plans to the point that we were, literally, unbeatable. The general agents who had been serving those grocers couldn't come close.

Becoming a **Buyer For** your customers, not a **Seller To** them, in a high-volume, established business system, is marketing's H-Bomb and fusion reactor. Here you will find all the power you'll ever want or need. It is a symbiosis.

CHAPTER 7

Close Encounters of the NEER™ Kind

THE SECRET CUSTOMER LIST

I don't know about you, but I've had enough theorizing for a while. It's time to take NEER out of this book and onto the street. First thing, though, you're going to look around your office. We're having a Treasure Hunt — one that deserves the name because what you're looking for may be, literally, a treasure for you and your business. It's buried right under your nose.

No, it probably isn't buried at all, but somewhere out in plain sight. Nobody, though, has thought to look inside of it for the treasure. It's been sitting there, untapped and unappreciated, for as long as your company has been in business.

- **Hint Number One** — What you're looking for is a list of potential customers.
- **Hint Number Two** — You can call on the people on the list with every confidence that you'll be listened to with the greatest respect and attention.
- **Hint Number Three** — You can be assured that these people are reputable, and their products and companies sound, because your own company puts its trust in them.
- **Hint Number Four** — Re-read the last section of Chapter 6.
- **Hint Number Five** — A riddle: When are you, the seller, also a valued customer?

The answer to the riddle is where the Treasure Hunt ends: You are a valuable customer when you're calling on someone on your own company's **accounts payable list.**

Whatever business you're in involves purchases from **suppliers and vendors,** who may be prime prospects for whatever you're **selling.**

Your **accounts payable** may well be your **dream calling list!** The companies on that list will receive you with open arms, and listen to every word you say, because your company is keeping them in business.

Prospecting your accounts payable is the first and easiest first-hand experience of the automatic, attention-getting power of the N_1 **NEER relationship.**

Everybody buys something from somebody, probably a lot of somebodies. This has been going on since Cave Man Number One paid Cave Man Number Two for a Sure-Kill DeLuxe Flint Spearhead. After a few million years, the idea of trying to **sell to** the folks you're **buying from** shouldn't be all that much of a surprise.

It is a surprise, though. Here at our seminars at Canyon Springs Ranch it strikes some of the very brightest business people like a bolt out of the blue. At least 99 percent never conceived of such a thing. The normal reaction, after How 'Bout That! is a moment or two of resistance, while the re-active parts of the brain think up reasons why calling on vendors won't work. Hesitation can't last, though, because more than 99 times out of 100 there isn't the shadow of a reason why it won't work. The only reason that it isn't **already** working is that nobody thought to try it, or tried only sporadically.

Not too long ago we explained this concept at a training session with a law firm. When the training was over, those attorneys practically ran out of the room, so they could start offering their services to the people who sold things to the firm. Office-machine companies, temporary-help agencies, decorators, bankers, janitorial services and landscapers — **everybody** to whom those lawyers wrote checks suddenly looked like fair game for a presentation. The firm immediately put this powerful prospecting tool to work.

Think about what your suppliers might do for **you**, if you called on them and asked. After all, your company is already doing a lot for them. The suppliers should already be thinking along the same lines, about what they can do to help you build your business. They ought to be thinking that way because they want to keep doing business with you, and have that business grow, because your company is growing.

Never, ever lose sight of this when you're dealing with your own customers:

Always do everything you can to help your clients grow.

• You'll build **trust** and **loyalty**, which gives you the high ground, against the competition.

• You'll **increase sales**, because if the customer's growing, he or she will buy more of what you sell.

We're getting ahead of the game, though. At this point you ought to be looking at your own accounts payable, and exploring this new territory of potential customers.

Imagine that your business is carpets. Who on your company's accounts payable is **not** a potential buyer? They all have floors, haven't they?

If you're a pavement contractor, chances are that some of your company's suppliers are walking or parking on potholes and cracks. They need your services, right now.

There are, of course, a few cases where this sort of reciprocal marketing won't work. The companies that sell upholstery to Boeing probably don't need commercial airliners. Suppliers to certain defense contractors don't want nuclear subs and anti-tank missiles. The exceptions are surprisingly few, though. Most buyer-seller relationships are potentially two-way.

With multiple NEER relationships and referrals, to multiply your reach, the **whole world's** accounts payable become your list of prospects!

This vein, which starts in your own business, is one of the greatest untapped resources in marketing. The place to start following the vein, and mining it, is where you work.

Am I hearing some objections? (Fair's fair — if you can read my book, I can listen to what you're thinking about it.)

Somebody just said, "Come on, Hailey, get real. I'm supposed to call on Acme Welding, and try to sell wall-to-wall carpets for their offices, just because they work on our vans? I doubt if we're doing $7,500 a year with Acme."

The answer is Yes! You absolutely should call on them.There's a good chance that the competition isn't doing **any** business with Acme. You've probably got a persuasive edge here. If you've **got** it, you'd better **use** it.

This brings us to one of selling's ultimate edges, a technique that will make you even more welcome when you call on supplier/prospects. This is the salesperson's equivalent of a diplomatic passport. It dissolves formalities, and lifts all the barriers between you and whoever you want to see. Don't be surprised if it gets you invited to lunch.

But saying it straight out is too easy. Try to guess:

- **Hint Number One** — The technique in question involves a piece of paper.

- **Hint Number Two** — For getting the prospect's immediate attention and respect, this piece of paper will outperform full-color brochures, flip charts and state-of-the-art electronic multimedia. For free.

- **Hint Number Three** — It comes from more or less the same place where you found the hidden prospect list.

- **Hint Number Four** — If you don't pick it up and carry it, it will go from your company to the supplier/prospect by U.S. Mail.

Take your company's **check** to the company you want to call on! There is no better way to introduce yourself to someone with the leverage to make something happen for you.

If you're in a big organization, this will take a bit of intramural persuasion. Go through channels. First sell your own boss on the idea. (You might want to give him or her a copy of this book, with this section marked.) The boss will probably have to make the approach to Accounts Payable for you. Be confident, though — a concept this good is bound to defeat the "We've never done this before!" mentality.

Once you've got permission, your boss will probably walk you down the hall, introduce you to Mr. or Ms. Bookkeeper, and explain that you are going to be delivering checks to some of the company's major suppliers. From Bookkeeping, find out how and where your company does its buying. Responsibility might lie with Purchasing, or maybe with the department that uses the product. After you know where the product is bought, talk to the person who buys.

Mr. or Ms. Buyer will be able to tell you something about the company on which you want to call.

Mr. or Ms. Buyer is your **external coach**, a very important character in our *Anatomy Of A Perfect Sale*. The **external coach** can answer your basic research questions and name his or her contact. We'll call this contact Stan Prospect Company's Seller – Stan PCS for short.

Once you know the **Seller**, who deals with your company's **Buyer**, you can call and say something like:

Persuader: Mr. PCS, my name is Bob Brown and I work at AdCo and I understand you work with Betty Buyer here.

Stan PCS: Why yes! Oh, Betty and I go way back.

Persuader: We're trying to create a better relationship with some of our suppliers and vendors, and I'm going to be meeting with some people over in your organization this week. I'd like to learn a little bit more about your company. Have you got a minute or two?

Does Stan PCS have a minute? Yes! Why? Because you are a customer.

At this point, Stan becomes an **internal coach**, within your prospect's company. Ask a few big-picture questions, about the prospect company in general, then focus on things of relevance to what you are selling.

Persuader: The program I have, which I'd like to tell your company about, involves market expansion through targeted multimedia campaigns. Tell me a little bit about who would be involved in that type of decision? Who's on the decision team? Who would be the key decision-maker?

Now you have the name(s) of your **prospect**. In our *Anatomy Of A Perfect Sale*, we list a short series of questions to ask, at this point. *Anatomy* details the sale itself, from **Hi** to **Buy**, and is the subject of another book.

In this volume we'll stick to the essentials: You must do research, and build a chain of referrals, to take you to whoever buys what you are selling.

If you don't do the research, your company's Bookkeeping will send you and the check to the other company's Accounts

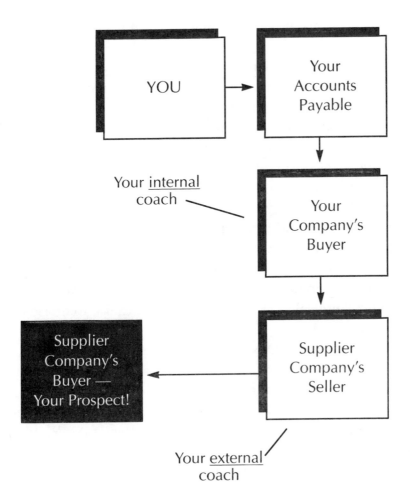

Build a chain of information and referrals to find your prospect and then call pre-heated.

Receivable, where Prince Charming himself will get no leverage, interest, or rapport.

Now, however, you have enough to get through your potential buyer's door, with enough information not to waste the Buyer's time asking ground-floor research questions.

You can call your prospect for an appointment:

Persuader: Mr. Prospect, I work for AdCo. As you know, our art department buys hydraulic phase equipment from your company, and, believe me, AdCo is extremely pleased with it. I spent some-time with Stan PCS, at your company, and he tells me a lot of good things about you and your department. I'm going to be in your area, and what I'd like to do is hand-deliver our check over to you, and meet you. Then I'd like to learn more about your company, and bring you up to date on some new things that we're doing. Do you have your calendar handy? I can be there Wednesday or Thursday ...

Is he going to say, "No, stay away from my office! Why don't you just send the money over to accounts receivable, like you always do?"

Highly unlikely. Chances are he'll receive you with all the courtesy and attention due to a representative of a company that keeps his company in business. The persuasive power of the N_1 **buyer's side** approach makes you a VIP.

When you walk into the office, smiling and holding your company's check, compliment Mr. Prospect and the work he does, based on information from your **internal coach.** Then try something like:

Persuader: Mr. Supplier, we owe you an apology. Our companies have been doing business together for all these years, and nobody ever told you about our targeted multi-media program, which might offer you some savings, and better market penetration, too...

Where you go from here will vary with the circumstances. One very effective option is to offer to look over whatever product or service your competition is currently providing. Tell the prospect:

Persuader: I don't know if we can improve on this, but it won't take me long to find out. I'd like to see the facts and figures of your current program, and then take them back to the office and give them some study. If there were a way you could save money or get better value, I'm sure you'd want to know about it. On the other hand, if your deal's the best on the market, you'd probably be glad to know that, too. I'll let you know what I find. How does your daybook look on Monday?

This approach works well because you're helping, as much as selling. You're not pushing, so the prospect won't feel the need to resist. It **feels** safe, for both buyer and seller. It is, indeed, a very safe introduction for you, because most of the time the competition has left an opening for you. My own experience shows that competitors' programs can be beaten in pricing and improved in quality or service — or both — at least 70 percent of the time. When you come back with your company's facts and numbers, you will, by the time and effort you've spent, have **earned** the prospect's renewed attention. You can also make your presentation with new confidence, because you now **know** your program is better value than your competitors'.

However you proceed with this prospect, NEER will have gotten you farther, faster: First, the system pointed you toward a prospect you didn't know you had. Then it gave you a better initial reception that you would have gotten without NEER. This isn't a guaranteed sale, but it's a head start that only NEER can provide.

A **do** and a **don't**:

• **Do** your research, first within your own company, then the prospect's, to make sure you're calling on the right person. Remember what the wise man said: **Spend Not Your Influence Unwisely.** NEER is too good to waste.

•**Do not** be the least bit aggressive, or coercive. This should be the most low-key, friendliest call you can make. Anything more is a violation of courtesy and ethics. To paraphrase Teddy Roosevelt:

Speak softly, when you're carrying a big check! The check silently says everything that needs to be said about the relationship of your company and the prospect's — better than you could ever say it. So don't try.

Think for a moment about the wonderful bridge of psychological associations built by the check: You, the seller, who normally represent money going out the door, bring it **in**. This sweeps away one of the greatest causes of resistance, on the part of the prospect, to you and what you have to say.

I believe I'm picking up some more objections out there.

For many of you, NEER-style thinking and tactics may be a bit alarming, at first. Maybe it feels weird, or wrong or impossible.

Don't blame NEER for these feelings — blame our selling culture, which refuses to let yesteryear's worn-out methods go.

The quickest way to overcome whatever hesitation you're feeling is take NEER out and **try** it. The usual reaction, once you see what it can do, is to go crazy with it.

That, incidentally, is what you're about to do. Before you go running over to Accounts Payable, though, I want to tell a story:

Sometimes NEER, which I've lived by and taught for three decades, catches me by surprise. It works better than I thought it would, and it works where I never thought to try it.

A case in point is what happened shortly after Steve Anderson, our young go-getter from Utah, joined Planned Marketing Associates. Steve, who apparently thought we ought to practice more of what we were preaching, said he wanted to take our checks around to the vendors with whom we do business locally. Why not? was the general response. Nobody thought it would do any harm. But, then again, nobody thought it would do any good. Our accounts payable is small, and an amazing mismatch with our local vendors. We sell sales and management training to a high-powered, mainly metropolitan clientele. We buy llama feed and stuff to keep the cars running and the ranch-house roof from leaking.

But Steve wanted to try. And try he did, taking the checks to the feed store, the lumber yard, and the auto shop, telling the owners about what we do. There were no takers, until Steve got to the hardware store. The manager listened to the presentation, then said he was sorry, but all training decisions in his company are made at headquarters.

Steve said he understood, and asked another question:

Now that you've met me and you know what we do, let me ask you this: Which one of your business contacts, who is involved in sales and marketing, might be a likely candidate for what we do?

The manager said his wife was involved in marketing at a company that sells private aircraft all over the world. Maybe that company would be interested.

Steve followed up on this, and the company turned out to be a very attractive prospect. He got a "No" on the first call, but put the 15 System to work. Turns out he had to make several calls before he got his Yes! He got it, though, and the president of the aircraft company came to one of our seminars.

This story illustrates a few very valuable lessons:

• Never get in the way of another person's enthusiasm.

• Never, ever leave a prospect without asking him or her to prospect for you. Ask for the name of someone else who might be a candidate for what you're selling.

• NEER works!

If it works here in the Hill Country, in the hardware store, it will work for you!

ACTION PLAN

NEER™ in Action

Time to take your first ride on the **NEER N_1** relationship. If you can't **do** what you're reading about, we've been wasting paper and ink.

• Make your first NEER call on one of your, or your company's, suppliers, the one who looks like the best potential customer. If possible, deliver the check.

• All the instructions you need are in the section you just read.

• Relax! You'll be welcomed as you never were before. This may well be the most stress-free call you've ever made.

• Debriefing: What was the outcome?

_____

_____

_____

• How were you received?

_____

_____

• What is the next logical step with this new prospect?

_____

_____

• Did the prospect name other potential customers?

_____

_____

• More analysis: From what you now know, does this prospect fit your 80/20 profile of a prime customer?

_____

_____

• What activities will be most effective for getting the sale?

_____

_____

_____

- What further intelligence do you need to help you proceed?

  _____

  _____

  _____

- Where/how will you get it?

  _____

  _____

- When are this prospect's **7 to 1** prime-buying hours?

  _____

  _____

  _____

- Rough out a **15 System** calling plan.

  _____

  _____

  _____

- Once you're up and running with this new prospect, try another. Then another. Remember to give each new prospect the benefit of all your analytical and persuasive techniques: **80/20**, **7 to 1**, and the **15 System**.

Your Favorite Customer

This exercise sets us up for the next section. At first it will be a thought problem, with written answers. In a few pages, though, you'll be taking action. So think carefully.

- Mentally review your current client list, and think of a customer who is particularly satisfied with you and your product, with whom you've been doing business for a while. This won't necessarily be your biggest customer, but he or she might be your **favorite**.

• The right person will be someone you like, who likes you, with whom you'll be comfortable discussing something slightly outside of the business you normally do together.

• This person, to qualify for the rest of the exercise, must be doing substantial business with other suppliers. If your first pick seems economically isolated, pick a second- or third-favorite who's part of a NEER flow. Example: A solo pianist is probably out, even if you're his or her daughter's godparent. The owner of an auto parts store would probably be a much better choice. Think **NEER connections**.

• Write the name of your first choice who meets the above requirements.

_____

• If you don't have a satisfied customer who fits the bill, pick one who comes closest.

_____

• If you don't have one single satisfied customer, you might consider a career change. You might consider becoming a cloistered monk.

• Recall the date and circumstances of your first sale to this person. Why did you consider him or her a prospect?

_____
_____
_____

Why has your business relationship been particularly satisfying for you?

_____
_____
_____

• Call and make an appointment to see the customer you just selected. Soon, but not right away; between now and then you need enough free time to read and digest the next two sections.

Try asking like this:

I've got an idea I'd like to share with you, and get some of your insight and input. It will take me only a few minutes.

This appointment call is a pretty good test of the relationship with your customer. Your relationship should be open to this sort of request. If it isn't comfortable to ask, you might be calling the wrong person.

Upstream NEER™ Navigation

Your first NEER encounter, where you called on one of your company's suppliers, brought into play the power, real and implied, of your position as a **customer**. In our Atomic Theory of NEER, this was an N_1. Your influence was flowing in the same direction as the money.

Would it make much difference if you **never** met this prospect previously, or if you were **not** introduced by someone with influence? Probably not, because you arrive with the ultimate calling card — a check made out to the buyer's company. If the check isn't there physically, it's there in spirit, which is almost as good.

A first approach from the N_1 side reminds me a little of that line from *The Godfather,* "Make him an offer he can't refuse." Your offer to spend a few minutes with a supplier/prospect is very difficult for him or her to refuse, when you're coming as a valued customer. You might say this initial N_1 approach is refusal-proof. This is a megawatt "Hello."

Sooner or later, though, the direct N_1 linkages run out. Your company only has only so many suppliers. Only so many of them will buy what you're selling. The business you turn up with this initial prospecting may be very valuable, but it's finite, and it stops pretty close to home.

Your potential NEERs, though, are infinite — or so vast that they might as well be infinite. You'll never exhaust them in one working lifetime.

A while ago I compared NEERs to rivers on the economic map. The easiest trips for beginners are downstream, following the flow of money. You just took such a trip.

NEER prospecting cannot, however, begin and end with basic N_1s, any more than barge traffic can run only downstream on the Mississippi. You've got to learn upstream — N_2 — navigation. At first this seems a bit trickier, but it opens up the entire business world. When you're an experienced NEER navigator, you can go wherever you want.

Our first N_2 **upstream** voyage will take you to the **customer** you identified in the last Action Plan. From that customer, you make a N_1 **downstream** cruise to call on one or more of the customer's **suppliers**, with the customer's endorsement.

Take a minute to review the last Action Plan, where you identi- fied a customer with whom you are particularly comfortable, who has multiple buying-and-selling connections.

The Action Plan questions, and the answers you gave, tell a lot about the dynamics of this relationship, and why and how an N_2 differs from an N_1.

(If it isn't clear to you why going to a customer is an N_2, and **not** an N_1, you'd better re-read The Atomic Theory of Business. We'll wait for you right here.)

Why, when you approach a customer, are your business history and personal relationship so important?

• They're important because **Trust** and **Respect**, not **Money**, is what cements your relationship with a customer. You must have **earned** a good deal of **Trust,** to ask what you're about to ask.

Both kinds of elemental NEER — N_1 and N_2 — give the person you contact a basic, compelling reason to receive you with courtesy and listen with interest. These basic, compelling reasons to pay attention are the glue that holds NEER relationships together.

But N_1s and N_2s use different kinds of glue, as different as Elmer's and Duco.

• In an N_1, when you're a customer, or calling with a customer's endorsement, what cements your position is primarily the **money** represented by the NEER relationship.

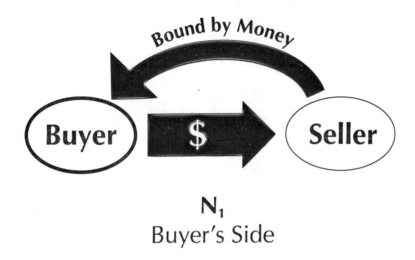

N_1
Buyer's Side

• In an N_2, where you're the supplier, or approaching with a supplier's endorsement, the critical force is the customer's long-standing **Trust** in the supplier.

Remember that we're talking ground-floor basics here, at the very beginning of NEER relationships. We're talking, in effect, about saying "Hello." In a maturing NEER relationship, trust becomes increasingly important in the N_1, and money in the N_2. Indeed, after a point, both kinds of NEER operate in all your business relationships, as what were once simple — and relatively fragile — selling and buying relationships become complex, mutually

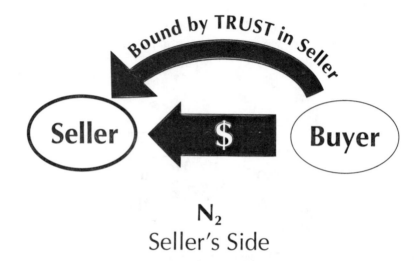

N_2
Seller's Side

beneficial, secure **strategic alliances**. Everybody builds **Trust**, because everybody is helping everybody else make **Money**. In an up-and-running NEER, you, the seller, become as valuable to your buyer as his or her best employee. You might as well be an employee, partner or major stockholder, because you've put your customer's best interests first, **Buying For** rather than **Selling To**, doing everything you can to make the customer's business grow.

Dress Rehearsal

Much as I hate written-down spiels, I want you to learn the following lines. Not word-for-word, but in **essence**. A successful N_2 NEER prospecting call on a **customer** has a few components that are absolutely vital. You will, naturally, have to speak in your own words, but you must make the right moves, in the right order.

First Move: Reversing Roles With Your Customer

You arrive for your appointment. After a short exchange of appropriate greetings and pleasantries, you begin the purposeful part of the visit.

You: In case you're wondering why I came by today, I've decided to concentrate on the quality side of my client base. My numbers have been showing me this is where the growth potential really is. When I started thinking about the customer relationships that have been best for me, you were the first person I thought of. What I'd like to do, is take you back about three years ago, when we first started working together, and ask you a couple questions.

Customer: I don't have a problem with that at all.

You: Do you remember the first time I called on you?

Customer: Why sure. We were still over at the old office.

You: You had a couple initial concerns, didn't you. (Recall those concerns.)

Customer: Well, yes, as a matter of fact. We'd been dealing with that other company for years.

You: Maybe you could go back, in your mind, and tell me what I did that you thought was effective, that helped you make your decision to buy from me. I'm talking about what I should be absolutely sure to duplicate, with other prospects of your caliber.

Customer: I remember you were very polite, even after I told you there probably wasn't anything for you here. And I liked the way you seemed to be very interested in our business, and to know a lot about it.

You: (Making notes) So interest and knowledge meant a lot to you...

From here on, prompting the buyer's memory, you briefly relive that first encounter and find out what it was — about you, your presentation, your product — that persuaded the buyer to say "Yes! I'll take it" for the first time.

This might seem like a strange, sideways sort of start for a meeting. But everything here happens for a sound psychological reason:

- It's important to begin by **asking for help**. People like you better, and are more receptive, when you appeal for assistance and they think they're giving it. I don't know why this is so, but it is. Philosophers and psychologists have been pointing out this fundamental human truth for centuries. You can't abuse the universal desire to help. People quickly recognize, and despise, a parasite. But "Can you help me?" is one of the world's most compelling openers.

- When the buyer, with your prompting, relives your first sale, he or she is, in effect, **re-selling you** to himself or herself. Referring to the client's initial resistance makes this psychological re-selling more powerful, as does echoing and feeding-back what led the client to choose you and your product, the first time. This is far more effective than if you tried to re-sell yourself. Having someone else to do your bragging for you is always more persuasive — and more attractive — to others. Other folks braggin' on yew, as we Texans say, is also one of the principle strengths of the NEER system.

- Taking the buyer back to the first sale is more than a refresher course in appreciating you. The time travel is necessary because of how buyers perceive value. Studies have shown that value, in the customer's mind, is highest at the moment of the first sale. All the sensations of a good buy — triumph, gratification, relief that a decision has finally been reached — peak at that moment. Repeat buys are pretty much routine, without a lot of emotional juice. The only way to bring back that first "Yes! I'll take it," feeling is to return by way of memory.

- You may, if you listen carefully, gain some very valuable insights into your persuasive techniques. It never hurts to hear somebody else's assessments of your on-the-job performance, which might surprise you.

• The main purpose here isn't information, though, but **preparation**. You're laying the groundwork for the rest of the conversation, and some important requests you're about to make. You must lay this foundation, by appealing to the long-standing trust implicit in your NEER relationship, and having the customer rediscover the original enthusiasm for you and your product, for the rest of the meeting.

Second Move: Naming Names

The Q&A about your first sale to this customer is done. While you're both still feeling the glow of shared recollections, it's time to move to the main NEER business.

You: Thanks a lot for the analysis. What you've told me will be extremely helpful. You know what kind of relationship we've had. I'm sure there are other suppliers and vendors, with whom you work on a regular basis, who have the same kind of relationship with you. I'd like you to walk us through a few of them that come to mind, and see if there's anybody in that group, to whom you would be comfortable introducing me. We're talking about one of your suppliers who has needs and requirements like yours. And simply introducing me, and explaining some of the successes we've had.

Customer: Let me think about that a minute....Well, we've got SupplyCo, they're pretty good people, and they might be interested.

You: Terrific, I've been wanting to call on them. Who do you do business with over there?

This scenario plays as many ways as people do business. But the principles are the same in all businesses, large and small, blue-collar and white-collar, at all levels. You ask for a referral only after establishing the necessary trust, and then ask in a way that doesn't invite **dis**trust. You ask, moreover, in such a way that makes it very easy for the customer to **answer**.

The best way to show what's right about this approach is to show you how to ask wrong:

Wrong Way #1

Sally Stockbroker: Who could you introduce me to, who I could talk to about investments?

If Ms. Stockbroker tries this "Who can I sell to?" approach without preparation, the meeting will stall, because she hasn't earned permission, in the customer's mind. Even if she does prepare, by going back to the first sale, asking outright to meet a prospective buyer is risky. For all sorts of reasons, it just doesn't **feel** right, for either Sally or her client.

The right way — **the NEER way** — the seller earns permission and appeals to the **relationship** with the customer, then asks about **duplicating that relationship** with someone else. This is much more comfortable to both parties, and much more likely to bring the seller a good referral.

Wrong Way #2

Dan Drummer: Who do you know who might be interested in me and my product?

Salespeople wanting referrals have asked this question millions of times — and millions of times their customers have drawn a blank. No, they say, they can't think of anybody, out of 250-some million Americans, who might be interested. Amazing, isn't it? With all this seeming **dis**interest in doing business, you'd think we still lived on roots and lizard haunches.

The problem isn't really disinterest — it's Dan Drummer's question, which is much too open-ended. In wording and psychology, it's all wrong, because it doesn't make the customer think about any particular group of people. Focus on a group, though, and suddenly the customer can call up faces and names, from which it's much easier to make a choice.

Ralph Moten, our expert in Presentations here at Planned Marketing, has a saying: Give them a **choice**, not a **chance**. Choices involve restricting and focusing alternatives. Wrong Way #2 gives your customer a wonderful chance **not** to answer. Almost any sort of **choice** is better than an open-ended **chance**. Always ask "Which one of..." then name a finite, easily-identified group, when you're asking someone to pick something out for you.

You're probably better off asking the customer about hazel-eyed people born under the sign of Taurus than to pick from the wide, wide world of anybody!

Of course our choice is hardly arbitrary. You're asking about the customer's **suppliers** for exactly the same reason you made your first NEER call on your company's suppliers — because this is the easiest first contact, with the **most automatic influence**, and the **least** feeling of **risk** and **discomfort**. Even if your customer doesn't understand the easy-flowing, low-risk N_1 relationship, he or she will **feel** it, and will be more comfortable making a referral.

Third Move: Making It Happen

So far, so good. You've got the name of a new prospect. Now is the time to do a little research. Ask a half-dozen questions about the prospect's business, and your customer's contact at that company. Learn what you can to help position yourself for a call. It may be, as we showed in the call on one of your company's suppliers, that you'll have to build a chain of NEER contacts. Your customer tells you about the prospect company's **seller**, who becomes an **inside coach** and tells you about the **buyer**, who is **your prospect**.

But questioning your customer shouldn't take more than a few minutes. Brevity, as the Bard says, is the soul of wit. It's also the soul of effective meetings. Finish this research segment on a **personal** note, talking about the customer's contact at the supplier.

You: This Will Bigdeal sounds like somebody I'd love to meet.

Customer: Yeah, he's a terrific good guy. And he can tell you more about SupplyCo than anybody.

You: I've got a brochure and spec sheets here. Maybe you could write a little note, and send it to Mr. Bigdeal along with this material.

Customer: Well...

You: I know you're busy. I've got a copy of a very short testimonial, a couple sentences long, that another customer did for me. I could drop it off with Doris, your secretary, on my way out. It says that you're happy with our relationship, and that I'm going to call.

Customer: Glad to do it. I don't think that will be a problem at all. Just give it to Doris, and tell her I want it on my letterhead this afternoon.

What you just read is a **best case scenario:** You leave your customer's office with a referral going out in that day's mail, after a minimal imposition on your customer. Wait another day, and you can call on your new prospect, Mr. William T. Bigdeal at SupplyCo, with every assurance that you'll be heard with courtesy and respect, because of your connection with one of his company's valued customers. I've done this thousands of times, and I can't remember being turned down. In the unlikely event that somebody does say No!, you're no worse off for trying, are you?

I recommend getting your sample referral note to the secretary, while you're still in the office, because it moves the NEER referral from **To Do** to **Done**, fast and very easily. The entire burden of the meeting has been discharged in one sitting. If you do it right, the whole business — from "Hi" to dropping the letter off with Doris — takes no more than 7 minutes. Your customer will never have the feeling that he or she has been imposed upon. The customer will, indeed, like you better, because it feels good to help, particularly when helping is so effortless.

Never forget to take the **initiative** and take — and keep —the **responsibility** for the follow-through on this NEER referral. This isn't pushing the customer, so much as accepting a burden, to make things easier for both of you. After all, he or she has no compelling, bottom-line interest in the referral. Once you're out of sight, and out of mind, the tendency is to back-burner it and, eventually, to forget it. This isn't a reflection on Human Nature so much as Business Nature — one's own business always comes first.

A vague commitment to contact the prospect — "Sure, I'll drop Will a line as soon as I can" — is about as useful as one of those "Let's have lunch sometime" invitations. Don't hold your breath.

An uncompleted referral can actually damage your relationship with your valued customer. This little-bitty deal, when it's unresolved, becomes a mutual irritant: You are irritated because you can't call on this new prospect. If you're reduced to reminding, and nudging the customer along, he or she will be irritated because it seems as though you're pestering.

Remember this:

• A prospect's name, in the NEER System, is not nearly as effective as a direct communication about you and your product from someone important to the prospect.

• Make it happen **now**! Everyone involved will be happier.

Depending on the circumstances, recommendations can take other forms.

Maybe your customer is about to see the prospect in person, and you know, on the basis of your relationship, that he or she can be counted on to mention you. You will want to give the customer a brochure, to take to the prospect. This material serves as a reminder, and gives a tangible focus to the short mention of you.

Once in a while your customer will offer to call the prospect, while you're still there. This can be great. But, if the prospect's not in or the line is busy, the follow-up can go into limbo, or worse,

Mutual Irritation-Land.

Remember that the trick is to take the burden **off** your customer. You might offer to take a sheet or two of the customer's letterhead and have the referral typed at your office, then bring it back for the customer to read and sign. Whatever you can do to speed the process — within the comfortable limits of your relationship — is all to the good.

When you show the customer a sample note, show him or her a **short** one. Here's another case where brief is beautiful. All the referral needs to say is that the customer is very satisfied with you and your product, that he or she thought the prospect might be interested, and that you are going to call. A few additional good words won't hurt. Anything beyond that, though, gets in everybody's way.

Sample typewritten referral from Satisfied Customer:

Dear (Prospect),
I've worked with (your name) for (approximate time) and we've enjoyed a very productive business relationship.

Enclosed you'll find some information about (brief description of your product or service). I suggested that (your name) give you a call.

When he (she) does, spend a few minutes with him (her). You'll like what you hear.
Sincerely,
(Satisfied Customer)

The ultimate no-pain approach is to show the customer a brochure and ask him or her to jot down a few sentences on a piece of memo-paper or even a stick 'em note. Then put the brochure and note in an envelope, address it, and use one of **your** postage stamps. Mail it yourself.

In a few cases, your Satisfied Customer won't want to send a note, but doesn't mind letting Mr. Prospect know that Satisfied Customer told you about him. In that case you can send the note. Again, short and sweet is best.

Sample Seller's referral letter:

Dear (Prospect),
(Your Satisfied Customer's Name) had great things to say about you and your organization and suggested that I send you some information about what we're doing together. We've shared some big successes, with this program.
I'll contact you in a few days to make sure you've gotten everything.
Sincerely,
(Your Name)

Enemies Within

I wouldn't be surprised if what you're reading makes you nervous. Right now you've got these timid, worried little voices in your head, whining about how they wouldn't feel quite right making this sort of request for help, to a customer, of all people.

The most common objection to this system is that asking a customer to help you find other customers might send an incorrect, very damaging message — that you, your company, or both, are desperate for new business.

Desperation can, indeed, be fatal. Start acting desperate and pretty soon your customers will give you something to be desperate about. Buyers want to feel, above all, **confident** in you and what you provide.

But **nothing** in the approach we've outlined for you even hints at desperation or trouble on your end. You are consulting a valued client, about a thought-through, sound program to expand your business. If anything, this client ought to be more confident in you after the meeting, which is flattering to both of you. It shows you in a good light, and shows, too, how valuable this business relationship is to you.

Logically, the reluctance to use this NEER technique doesn't have a leg to stand on. Reluctance doesn't need logic, though. In this case, the reluctance is really FEAR trying to act intelligent. But FEAR, whether or not it's using a big vocabulary, or trying to pass itself off as common sense, is still FEAR.

Here at Hailey ranch, FEAR is — what else? — an acronym:

False

Evidence

Appearing

Real

Much of time this is all fear is.

Of course, the evidence isn't always false. If, for instance, you pull into a client's parking lot at the crack of dawn, and the guard dogs are still running around, you might want to stay in your car. With doberman pinschers, you've got **F**erocious **E**vidence **A**ctually **R**eal! You can say the same for trucks coming at you head-on, runaway trains and sitting on somebody's cowboy hat in the wrong bar in Lubbock.

If, on the other hand, you're afraid to call on a trusted, long-time client for a few minutes' assistance, which won't cost a thing, something is definitely **False!**

The problem is entirely imaginary, and now is the time to do something about it.

If you don't do something about it, it will be hard, if not impossible, to lift your selling performance above the mediocre.

Turn back to this book's first chapter, **Programming The Two-Billion-Dollar Computer**, if you're seriously squeamish about making a NEER contact through one of your customers. You're probably feeling shaky about one or more of the **Three Ps: Person — Profession — Process.** Shakiness will become solidity when you rediscover your confidence in the **Value & Integrity** of yourself, what you're selling, and being a seller, and are thoroughly confident in the way you prospect and sell.

In selling, fear and lack of confidence result in what we term **Call Reluctance** (**CR** for short) or **Activity Avoidance** (**AA**) where you're reluctant to do anything at all. Consciously or subconsciously the Call-Reluctant Persuader doesn't want to face buyers — prospective buyers or, sometimes, current buyers. Here at Planned Marketing we've observed that the most severe form of Call Reluctance is the inability to face one's own customers and ask for referrals. Strange, but true.

A Call-Reluctant Persuader is a painful contradiction — like a gun-shy professional marksman, or an ironworker who's afraid of heights. But the Call Reluctance is also typical. CR is absolutely epidemic in this business. Persuaders suffer from it the way coal miners used to suffer from black lung.

Take heart, though. If CR has been hurting you and holding you back, you're reading the right book. This system nips CR in the bud. Gone forever are the heartbreaking, humiliating aspects of selling that cause you to dread calls. Never again will you have to work up the courage to approach somebody who doesn't know you from Adam (or Eve), who doesn't have a reason in the world to hear you out with courtesy and respect. NEER, if you understand it, and use it and give it half a chance, **cures** Call Reluctance, once and for all.

Of course reading this won't convince you. What will convince you is trying it. And that, once again, is what you're about to do.

ACTION PLAN

- You've got an appointment with one of your favorite customers.
- You've got a script that shows how to get from "Hi" to a referral to a solid new prospect. The formula will, most likely, get you a written endorsement from the customer before your meeting is over.
- Learn the **moves**, not the **words**. Remember to:
    - Begin by asking for help.
    - Ask the customer to re-live the first sale, to re-sell you to himself or herself.
    - Appeal to this relationship when you ask for a referral. You're asking to duplicate the relationship you and your customer have.
    - Give a **choice**, not a **chance**. Ask, "Which one of your suppliers..."
    - Research. Ask a few questions about the prospect. Get the **name** of someone known to your customer.
    - Make the referral happen now! Give a sample letter to the secretary, or whatever it takes — within the comfort zone of your relationship with your customer.
    - Remember that you cannot call on the prospect until the customer has completed the referral.
    - Show your appreciation! First with a big, bright Thanks! at the end of the meeting. Then let the customer know what's happening, particularly if things go well with this new prospect.

• Debrief Yourself, After Meeting With Your Customer:
How were you received?

_____

Any surprises? _____

_____

What was the outcome?

_____

If the referral was not made during your meeting, what was
its status when you left?

_____

How will you make sure the referral is made, in a timely
fashion?

_____

On a scale of 1 to 10, rate how worthwhile this meeting was.

_____

What would have made it better?

_____

What will you do different next time?

_____

• Call on your new prospect, and use your all your analytical, planning and persuasive techniques — 80/20, 7 to 1 and the
15 System. Read your instruments, believe them and **fly** by them
until you hear "Yes! I'll take it."

Variations on the Theme

Canyon Springs Ranch is not what you'd call an in-town location. The folks from San Antonio have to spend an hour-and-a-half

on the Interstate to get here. Of course most of our seminar participants come from much farther away than SA. To make their journeys worthwhile, we try to pack in as much information and inspiration as we can, concentrating 40 years of professional experience into three days. You don't come here to catch up on your sleep, or do a lot of daydreaming. But the people leave much more energized than they arrive. The seminar puts much more bounce in them than a weekend lying around on the beach. Rest may not be the best cure for the weary.

But you've got to allow for the limits of the human attention span. We've made a science out of keeping things moving, with shifts of mood and regular breaks, to keep everybody wide-awake and thinking. When the circulation starts to get sluggish, and the brain fog rolls in, everybody gets on their feet. Then we all shout sayings posted on the seminar room walls, while we massage each others' necks and shoulders. After the noise and the neck-rub we get a quarter hour for coffee, some fresh air and Nature's calls.

One of things we shout is this:

When the student is ready, the teacher appears!

This sentence is much longer in wisdom than words. It shows one of the universal truths behind our system: Chances are that what you **want** to happen is **waiting** to happen. But it can't happen until you're **ready** for it. The most important work you do is getting ready. Preparation, as just about every great person in history has shown us, in words and by example, is most of success. NEER isn't about selling, so much as it is about getting **ready** to sell, which can be much more important to your success than the presentation and close.

"When the student is ready..." reminds us, too, that if you want to learn something, somebody, somewhere wants to teach it to you. If you look, and listen and read, pretty soon the mentor you need will appear.

You can turn the saying around: When the **teacher** is ready, the

student appears. The exchange of valuable ideas always runs both ways. Many of our seminar participants leave just as much as they take.

This happened not too long ago, when a woman came up with a terrific way to combine the first two NEER techniques. She called and told us about it after her weekend at the ranch.

In this chapter, as you recall —

First, you used your own accounts payable as a prospecting list.

Second, you called on a customer and got a referral to one of the customer's suppliers.

Both ways you came at the prospect from the same direction as the money, riding on the shoulders of a buyer-to-seller N_1 relationship. On the first call the money came from your company. On the second call, it was your customer's. The effect, though, was similar. You were welcomed, and listened to.

Our student had the bright idea of going straight to the customer's accounts payable, thereby gaining multiple referrals from a single meeting!

Of course this takes some finesse. Her appointment call goes like this:

Ms. Highlighter: Mike, I was just at a sales seminar, and I picked up an idea that I think will help your company expand its markets. It won't cost you anything to find out about it. Have you got a few minutes?

Mike: Sure.

Ms. Highlighter: Well, what we'll need is your company's accounts payable list. Now I want you to be sure and scratch out anything you or anybody else deems confidential. All we need is your suppliers' and vendors' names.

She arrives to find Mike and his accounts payable — with the dollars-and-cents details inked out. She puts two highlighters, one yellow and one orange, on the desk. Then she says that she and Mike are going to go through the list and see if there are any good prospects for Mike's company's products that are not currently being pursued. She tells Mike the yellow marker is for marking these new prospects.

In one sitting, our fluorescent marker genius identified **more than 20** good prospects for her customer!

After targeting the customer's prospects, she tells a little about NEER marketing and the accounts payable approach. Then — this is the good part! — she says:

"Now you're probably wondering what this orange highlighter is for..."

It is, of course, for marking those vendors and suppliers on the list that are likely prospects for her.

Does the customer mind if she picks up some leads and asks for referral notes? Of course not! Why not? Because Wonder Woman just showed him a whole bunch of potential business, and gave him some excellent advice on how to get it. Mike gets a substantial benefit before she asks for the favor.

And the two markers are sheer brilliance! This is one of those little details that makes the process go. You'd have a hard time explaining why, but the markers make it better.

Of course her approach would work without markers. It would work because the customer is more than repaid for the time and trouble. Quid Quo Pro is always a sound basis for productive dialogue. Give help, when you're asking for it.

You might consider bringing your own accounts payable list to this meeting, so the sharing is truly 50/50. Then you'll be in a position to give referrals, as well as get them.

Always remember to reassure the customer about what you need to know — company names only. All that matters here is this: You two are discovering new prospects to call on, with the endorsement of someone who supports the prospects' businesses.

NEER, when you use it like this, multiplies, rather than adds to, your list of qualified prospects, on whom you will call **warm**, rather than cold. You can easily generate pre-heated prospects faster than you can call on them.

Sometimes, though, you've got a single, special buyer in mind. In this case, use your intelligence-gathering to find out which one of your customers buys from the target. Then make the same sort of approach you've made — but instead of asking "Which one of your suppliers..." and so on, say that you've been wanting to meet so-and-so and take it from there.

If you don't have a customer who buys from your supplier, you can probably find an indirect link — somebody who buys from somebody else, who buys from your target. Somewhere your current buying-selling business relationships link you to your target. If you're patient, and take the time to forge strong intermediary links, you'll be welcomed into your target's office, because of the warm endorsement of one of that person's influencers. With that influence on your side, you'll be much more likely to hear "Yes! I'll take it."

Virtually any bit of intelligence can get you where you want to go. Let's say you want to call on the Jones Co., and one day you see a Jones Co. truck making a delivery to one of your customers. There's your NEER lead — go for it!

These principles work just as well way up in the executive suites and board rooms. Once I showed an investments broker how to call on a bank's board of directors. Instead of asking for business, he asked the board members who they knew who might want to buy their bank's stock. Did the board have a sound business reason to give him leads? You bet! They had every reason in the world to promote the sale of their company's stock. He got excellent referrals and introductions. The broker's business didn't end there, though. After asking the board members to help him promote their bank's best interests, the relationship deepened, and he got the bank's stocks and bonds business.

In a variation on this theme, I showed another broker how to sell stock through a company that his brokerage had just taken public. He approached the company right after its first public offering, and asked to see a supplier list. The company, naturally, wanted to know why. And he had a **gorgeous** answer: "Shouldn't your suppliers have an opportunity to experience the same growth that you and your stock have experienced?"

Did he get introductions to suppliers?

You tell me.

The motivation was the same as the bank board's. The company helped itself by helping him sell its stock. The suppliers, by investing, bound themselves more closely to their customer.

Whew, the air's getting a little thin up here. Before you buy your custom-made suit and mount your assault on high finance, you'll want to get the feel of NEER, with some more simple N_1 prospecting, like what you've done so far. This should be an exploratory phase.

We might call you a PioNEER, at this point. You must grow your business the way our forebears tamed the wilderness. Preparation — cutting trees and pulling stumps — was the hardest work. But the pioneers couldn't stop working when the land was cleared. No, they had to plant, harvest and keep their land fertile by taking care of it. If they meant to stay, and leave their children something worth having, they had to continuously re-invest in their land. If you mean to stay in business, you must expand the same, pioneering, step-by-step way, always remembering to take care of what you've started.

8

Elephants in the Living Room

SPEAKING THE UNSPEAKABLE

Much as we admire our ancestors, some of what they thought and did strikes us today as ludicrous. What they wouldn't do, to avoid giving offense, is downright hilarious. A hundred years ago a woman kept her ankles hidden, for fear of ruining her reputation. We call cooked chicken "white meat" and "dark meat" because old-time ladies and gentlemen could not utter such words as breast, leg and thigh. They could **eat** the poor chicken, but could not **say** what they were eating!

This is funny, but we shouldn't kid ourselves about the progress we've made toward total above-boardness. Hypocrisy and euphemizing — the $10 word for talking nice-nice, in order to avoid saying something disturbing — are as big as ever. Could be they're bigger than ever.

We live in the midst of huge things, big as barns and stomping around in broad daylight, which we do everything possible to ignore. If somebody **forces** us to acknowledge them, we refuse to call them by their names. And when somebody does speak the plain truth, we argue or cover our ears, even though we know the truth-tellers are right. Of course most of the time nobody is trying to point out the obvious. Denial is a group effort.

We all have an elephant in the living room!

Most of us have two or three. They scare the daylights out of us. It costs a fortune to feed them. They ruin the rugs. But we pretend they aren't there! Our houseguests never say anything, either, because they have their own. Nobody is talking, much less doing anything, about these pachyderms in the parlor!

Funny thing, though — the more you ignore them, the worse the situation gets. As the old proverb (which I just made up) says: He who denies the presence of a 6,000-pound tusker ruins many pairs of shoes.

Once you admit the thing is there, you can, at least, start cleaning up after it. After that you can train it, ride it away and donate it to a wildlife park. Once you're in control, the options are all yours.

So it always goes with denial. It gives power to whatever you're denying, and makes problems worse and worse. The end of denial — looking straight at the problem, and saying what it is — is the beginning of the solution.

Right now we're going to climb up on stepladders and take a look, square into the eyeballs, at two of the most powerful — and most universally denied — forces in persuaders' lives. We're going to call the things by their rightful names. Then we're going to show them who's boss. Welcome, friends and neighbors, to Hailey's Elephant Obedience School!

But you don't need to go back to your living room to start teaching your critters "sit" and "go fetch." They're right there with you, wherever you are — at the office, on an airplane, in a hotel room. We salespeople have particularly loyal elephants. They can't stand to let us out of their sight.

Dumbo Number One: Fear

You can only push a metaphor so far. Another few inches, and this one will turn around and attack. But I can't quit without that old story about the blind philosophers who felt different parts of an elephant and proclaimed, depending on what they took hold of, that an elephant is just like a snake, a rope, a tree and so on. We've been doing the same sort of thing with our first elephant — Fear. So far in this book, we have grasped it here and there, and talked about whichever part we had, without acknowledging the presence of the whole.

Back in the chapter about the 15 System, we talked about the Fear of No, which we counteracted by re-defining No as a Yes! waiting, and wanting, to happen. This, in fact, is just what it is, 9 out of 10 times, when you use the 15 System. A few pages ago, we touched on Call Reluctance, a symptom related to Fear of No but more generalized and serious. With Call Reluctance, you're not just afraid of what the buyers will tell you, you're afraid of buyers themselves, and put yourself through all sorts of contortions to stay away from them. And you can't just think your way out of this one, as you did with No-phobia.

CR and the fear that engenders it, are, unfortunately, the near-inevitable consequences of our prevailing selling culture. If you don't have CR to begin with, some time in the trenches will probably give it to you. A little bit of Cold Calling provides pretty good reasons to be terrified of leaving the office or picking up the phone. Nobody wants to be treated the way Cold Callers are treated. Look what it did to me! One little old pig farmer being rude when I was trying to sell him insurance brought on a total ego-collapse.

Of course, the pig farmer was also doing me a very big favor. He put me over the edge. Right then and there I got more angry (Fear's fightin' first cousin) and more afraid of having this happen again, than I was afraid of changing. I knew that I either had to quit what I was doing, before it flat-out destroyed me emotionally, or I had to **change** what I was doing. For about 12 hours I said I was going to quit. Then, with a little help from a mentor, I decided to stay in insurance sales. This meant I was deciding to change. The change was NEER. I went **From Fear to NEER** and never went back. Of course I still bump into my old buddy, Fear, from time to time — Mr. F. is as inescapable as breathing in and out and the IRS — but he can't get to me the way he used to, especially not in my professional life. These days I still get the occasional case of the jitters, calling on particularly famous people, but it's never serious enough to stop me.

From Fear to NEER is where you are going, right now. Never again will you depend on "a shoeshine and a smile" and the fragile basis of first impressions to try to make perfect strangers listen to you with respect. Once you've tried NEER, you will never go back to what you were doing before you tried it —unless, of course, you especially enjoy low pay, insecurity and insulting treatment. (If you do, you're way beyond the reach of this book.)

Fear lurks everywhere in this business: Beyond the fear of being turned-down, and the fear of making calls, there's fear of failure, fear of disappointing your spouse and kids and parents, fear of the boss, fear of young go-getters who want your job, fear of what the neighbors are thinking, even fear of success. There's something waiting to jump out and go "Boo!" wherever you turn. But they all, past a certain point, become one in the same: capital-F Fear, your Number One Bull Elephant.

When you think about it rationally, it seems odd that selling should be so frightening, and sellers fear-ridden. In terms of life-and-limb hazards, our profession is really very safe. But of course Fear has very little to do with rational thought and real danger. As Franklin D. Roosevelt said so memorably, "The only thing we have to fear is fear itself."

Fear usually does much more damage than whatever we're afraid of. Drinking, gambling, midnight hotel-room rambling — all the self-destructiveness and loose and erratic living with which the world identifies salespeople are the actions of people who are scared, who don't want to admit they're scared, and don't know what to do about it.

Think back to our acronym — False Evidence Appearing Real – and remember, please, that is the kind of fear we're addressing. Nobody is talking about enraged mama grizzlies and chemical plant explosions. There are plenty of things you'd better run from, if you want to live to finish this book. But what you do for a living is **not** one of them!

Every day is a misery, when you're afraid of your own productive work. You're afraid of calling on clients and prospects, so you avoid it with all sorts of make work, and fake work — rattling papers, calling friends on the phone, getting to the office late and taking too long for lunch. Sooner or later, though, fear of what will happen if you don't call on anybody overwhelms the fear of calling. So you call — but on too few buyers, too late. Or maybe you favor those who are nicest to you, whether or not they're good prospects. Either way, you can't do more than scrape by. So then you're afraid of failure, with good reason, because you're always too close to it.

All day you run from one thing, until another gets after you, then you run from that. You're running, but you don't get anywhere, because you're running in place. You're trying to hide, but there's nothing to hide behind.

Too many people are living this bad dream, refusing to wake up. Thoreau was talking about this kind of existence when he said, "The masses of men lead lives of quiet desperation."

They're quiet, because they won't even whisper to themselves what's really going on.

Thoreau also said, "Resignation is desperation confirmed."

What's **confirmed** can be **unconfirmed**. (Just ask anyone who does a lot of business flying.)

Now is the time to face the multiple, nagging fears that make you feel desperate, that have got you running' every which way, so you're not gettin' anywhere.

- Start with a simple admission: **I am afraid.**
- **Face** the things that make you afraid.
- **Name** those things. **Say** what they are.
- **Learn** what you can do about them.
- **Start doin' it now!**

There is no one-step, instant way to overcome our fears. The only instant remedies are fakes and poisons — like too many martinis, credit card binges and other pain-killers and foolish distractions. When the effects wear off, you are worse off than before.

What works is step-by-step **change**. You must learn new ways of thinking and new ways of acting. Education and action — **thinking and doing** — go hand in glove here.

Mastering our NEER system of marketing, which eliminates, once and for all, the most fearful things about our business, will probably feel like learning to swim. It starts out a little bit scary, but fear doesn't stand a chance, because NEER, like swimming, gets rewarding and fun so rapidly. The deep water, which used to scare the heck out of you, is suddenly a place to play.

You could tell a non-swimmer everything he needs to know about the front crawl stroke in fifteen minutes. The concepts of breathing, kicking and stroking are, after all, very simple. But if you threw him into the deep end of the pool after the lecture, he'd be in trouble. Nobody can learn to swim without practice in the water, and nobody can learn all at once. What works best are well-ordered sessions of learning and practice, moving on to the next step only after you're comfortable. The better you get, the less you're afraid, and the less you have to be afraid of. Pretty soon it's hard to believe you were **ever** afraid of the water.

Work on your NEER techniques and concepts the same way. Soon you will have a hard time believing that any part of this business once scared you.

Elephant Number Two

Number Two, as we're about to see, is sneakier than the first, and a master of disguises...

First, though, let's take a break. I want you to take a pretend phone call.

This is a very important call. Yesterday the White House Chief of Staff got in touch with the CEO of your company, who checked with your divisional vice-president to make sure that you were going to be in today, and that your line would be clear. Then Action News and the newspapers called up. All night your mother was burning up the wires, bragging to everybody in 8 states that her baby is expecting a call from the **President of the United States!**

The Chief Executive's message surprises you. After a little small talk he mentions that there's a salesperson who works in your area, representing the new line of Better Brands Something-or-Other, which the White House buys. The President happens to know that you buy this sort of product for your company, and thought you might benefit from meeting this seller and learning about the product.

You do, in fact, buy for your company. But you've had a deal with AAA Acme Something-or-Other since you started, your predecessor bought from Acme, and the bids from other companies never even come close. Not only that, you're engaged to somebody who works at Acme's District Office. The wedding is next week.

Oh, by the way, the President is saying, the salesperson for Better Brands happens to be sitting in the Oval Office, right now. Maybe you could make a 10-minute appointment. Which day next week is best? Is morning or afternoon better?

What are you going to say?

Are you going to turn down a request, made through the **Most Powerful Man in the World**, to sit down with somebody for only 10 minutes?

No, you're going to settle on a date and a time. Even though you have very little interest in the presentation, you'll listen to it. You'll listen even if the salesperson turns out to have scuffed shoes and bad breath, and no knowledge of the product at all.

Why do you take this meeting, and stay on your best behavior?

Because the President called you.

Would you have acted differently if somebody else called?

If you're like 99.999 percent of humanity, how you respond depends a great deal on who is asking you to respond. Let's say the guy who vacuums your office at night makes an identical approach, about someone he knows who sells the same product. You are far more likely to say, "Sorry, I appreciate the tip, but I'm just not interested."

What's going on here? Why — when two people offer exactly the same thing — do you say Yes to one and No to another?

While you're thinking about the answer, go back over this section and look for the Number Two elephant, which is hiding between the lines. If you look close, you can make the whole thing out, trunk, eyeballs, big ears and all. (You're right, I told a fib back at the beginning of the section, when I said we were going to let our elephants alone for a while. The idea was to allow Number

Two to sneak up on us.)

The answer to the question — why you say Yes to one person, and No to another, when they're asking exactly the same thing — is the Number Two Elephant. And, just as it appears in many guises, it goes by many names: **pecking order, hierarchy, status level, class, standing, prestige.**

You said Yes! to the President, even though you weren't particularly interested in what he proposed, because of his **rank** in a **pecking-order** to which you, as a citizen of the United States, belong. He **outranks** you. You, in turn, **outrank** the guy with the vacuum cleaner.

• In all human interactions, there is a **silent, secret caste system** at work.

• All other things being equal, this **caste system alone** will govern who does what, with whom.

Our hypothetical example — the President of the United States versus the cleaning person — seems unrealistic, if not ridiculous. But rank really works like this, even when we don't realize it is working.

We defer, and expect deference, according to standing in the psychological pecking order that governs each of our business contacts. We are always acutely, reflexively aware of hierarchical standing. We can't help it. Human beings are, it seems, built that way, as are all social creatures. The term pecking order comes from the barnyard, where you've got executive chickens that have the privilege of pecking paid-by-the-hour chickens. We higher, more elaborately social animals sometimes **act out** status differences, without getting physical. The struggle, sometimes symbolic, sometimes by lethal combat, is always the same, though — to establish **precedence**, and thereby have others **defer**. In the long view, there really isn't all that much difference between an office and a baboon troop.

Like everything else about humans, our hierarchical relationships are more complex than those of animals. Most people belong to many pecking orders, and are simultaneously higher on some, lower on others. A nobody at work might be a very big noise in the regional council of model airplane clubs. For building influence at his corporation, this relationship wouldn't be worth a thing. If, on the other hand, you own the local hobby shop, he is a Red Carpet VIP. In the world in which you do business, he is a prime influencer. What he does will likely be noticed, and copied, by others.

As you become more adept with NEER, and expand and fine-tune your prospecting, it becomes more and more crucial to recognize and work within the psychological pecking-orders to which your prime 80/20 prospects belong. Every city and town has easily identified business and social hierarchies — corporate, church, country club, charitable organizations — that can provide paths of approach. These are the routes to the right NEER contacts and referrals, particularly to build relationships with the wealthy and powerful.

At all socio-economic levels, high or low, the best NEER referral comes from a person your target perceives as important, as well as a valuable business relationship. The slickest NEER referral follows the money. It also comes from at least one perceived status-level above the person you're approaching.

When I directed and trained my own sales forces, I always hammered on the importance of pecking-order in prospecting. One guy absolutely failed to get it.

One afternoon he ran into my office, all excited. "I think I can get us the Dr. Pepper account," he said.

"That's great!" I said, "How are you going to do it?"

"Well, my new neighbor is a route driver for Dr. Pepper, and he can introduce us to the big guys!"

This man's idea was so bass-ackwards, it would have done us more harm than good!

Why wouldn't it work?

Because you don't normally meet executives to convince them to make an executive decision, such as buying an insurance program, by making an approach through uniformed, paid-by-the-hour, union employees. Why not? Because you don't. Period. Plain and simple. Business doesn't work that way because people don't work that way.

That contact with the Dr. Pepper driver might have turned out to be valuable if my salesman had done preliminary research, to find out who's who at the company. Then he could have worked out a plausible NEER approach. But he wanted to go waltzing into the company with the driver introducing him all around.

No, my guy didn't get it. He was like the fellow who asked the great trumpeter Louis Armstrong to explain jazz. Louis said, "If you gotta ask, you'll never know." Some people never get it, about the importance of hierarchies, and they never rise very far, particularly in sales. Make sure you get it, if you intend to succeed. Like it or not, there is always a psychological pecking order, a silent caste system, in every human organization. Learn it, and use it, and make it your friend.

We Americans have a hard time coming to grips with this. It is, really and truly, an elephant in the national front room, which we try very hard to wish away. People are afraid to talk about it. The great motivator Earl Nightingale, one of the few who isn't afraid to talk about it, said that we could do our children an enormous favor by teaching them about the socio-economic pyramid, so they could know how high they are now, and make clear life decisions about how high they want to go.

We are, however, reluctant to say such things out loud. The idea of hierarchy goes against our highly individualistic grain. It seems to betray a sacred founding principle of this country — that all humans are created equal.

But pecking-order has absolutely nothing to do with stature in God's eyes, or before the law, or in your eyes. The Maker loves and cherishes delivery men as much as CEOs. So should you. And the business world depends on good hourly people every bit as much as the folks with corner offices and $500 briefcases.

You, however, are not God. Nor are you the United States Constitution, or Society As A Whole. You can't make decisions about business relationships from such lofty heights. To meet the right people to refer you to the right people to make substantial purchases of your product, you must study the pecking orders to which your targets belong, and use them to get the referrals that will guarantee the best possible receptions.

• We're talking **practicalities** here, for meeting **specific people**, with **specific ends** in mind.

• These are never **judgments**.

The more you try to deny the existence and importance of pecking-order, the more power it has over your business life.

Those from more formal, class-dominated societies sometimes say that status issues cause us Americans terrible trouble, precisely because we try to deny them. I know a Japanese businessman who says he would much rather bow low to his department head, than call the boss Maggie or Bob and worry all day about how to show enough deference. In the Japanese system of protocol, you know what you're supposed to do, do it, and forget about it. In the American system, we can't forget about it, because we often have no idea what we're supposed to do!

Life gets much simpler when you learn to recognize and work within hierarchies. Your efforts count for more, because your influence is increased by prestige that is already widely recognized.

Borrowing Prestige

The cream always rises to the top — remember that old saying? It means, more or less, that you shouldn't worry about how you stand in others' eyes. Just do your best, and you will, inevitably, advance. It means, in other words, that Hailey is entirely **wrong** about pecking-order.

As with any old saying, there's some truth here: You should, indeed, be part of the cream, by always doing your best. Anything less is a betrayal of yourself, which you'll always regret. And cream does rise.

It rises **slowly**.

It rises so slowly that the farmers who make their livings selling dairy products use machines to separate milk and cream. They don't have time to wait for the cream to get to the top on its own.

Slowly is how you'll rise, all on your own. In 30 or 40 years, you might be eyeball-to-eyeball with anybody in the land, ready to do business as equals.

If you don't want to wait that long — I know I didn't — you must speed up the process.

The way to give yourself the prestige and influence you need is to **borrow** somebody else's.

When you approach a prospect with a referral from one of his or her best customers, you are borrowing the economic influence of that customer. Prestige can be borrowed in much the same way.

Back home in Mesquite, Texas, when I was getting my start in business, there wasn't all that much prestige to borrow. The only conspicuously successful person in my family's acquaintance was Ben Tisinger, who was a friend of my dad's. Just knowing Ben, the way Dad knew him, wasn't enough for me. I wanted to know what he knew and, especially, **who** he knew. I went to work for Ben's insurance company just at the moment when he needed a hard-charging seller. This also happened to be the moment that I needed mentoring about my new field.

Our relationship was particularly fruitful after working hours, because Ben made me his unofficial chauffeur.

This wasn't Ben's idea — it was mine.

Since neither Ben nor his wife liked to drive at night, I volunteered to take them to dinner parties and other evening functions of the rich folks and high achievers. Unlike a real, paid-by-the-hour chauffeur, I went inside as Ben's guest, gaining entry where I wouldn't have had a prayer on my own, meeting people I never could have met without "Mr. Ben" as folks around Mesquite called him back then.

Ben showed me what's fashionable about "fashionably late." He liked to arrive at dinners a minute or two after everybody sat down. When we walked in, where do you think everybody's head turned? They had to notice us: "Oh look, there's Ben," they'd be telling each other. And then, "Who's that little guy with him?"

People who saw us together started making approaches through me: "You know, I'd really like to meet that Ben Tisinger." Whether or not they got to know him, they got to know Walter Hailey!

This was one of my first experiences in borrowed prestige. Our deal worked because I always paid interest on what I borrowed. If I hadn't driven, Ben would have missed many of his evening functions. Benefits must always be reciprocal in such relationships. Wealthy and accomplished people are especially sensitive to parasites, who want to be close to them just for the thrill, or want something for nothing. They are, by the same token, particularly grateful to those who are genuinely interested in them, who have something of value to offer.

Remember this: There is absolutely no point pursuing Mr. and Mrs. Bigdeal unless you have a sound business motive, with a solid benefit for yourself, along with something worthwhile to offer them. Prestige and money are never going to come off on you, if all you're doing is rubbing shoulders.

I had very sound reasons for wanting to meet the wealthy and up-and-comers in Mesquite and East Dallas. My business was financial services. I would, naturally, do better if I sought out those who had more finances to service. And, although they didn't know it at first, those people had excellent reasons to want to meet and do business with me. The deals I made always had powerful benefits for my customers.

Long before anybody was talking about Win-Win deals, I was doing them, and nothing but. I didn't work this way because I was a wonderful guy — I did it because this is a wonderful way to work. If you want to build solid, and reap the biggest personal and financial rewards, it's really the **only** way to do business!

I wish everything I did, to advance my own cause, was as painless as going to fancy dinner parties with Ben Tisinger. A few times I had to go way out on a limb to get where I wanted to be, among the people I wanted to be with. Getting into the rich folks' country club took every penny I had. I even had to cash out of my stock option plan from Burrus Mills.

I'd never even been in a country club until I joined. All I knew about it was that the rich folks were members, which was all I needed to know. I immediately started doing business over breakfast there. It didn't cost any more than breakfast at Joe's Restaurant, and it made a much better impression.

In those starting-out years I had to borrow the money to buy enough stock to get on the local bank's board of directors. I even formed a Rotary chapter in Dallas' White Rock area. I couldn't get into the one in my home town of Mesquite, because a competitor in the insurance business belonged to the Mesquite Rotary.

I had the first meeting all by myself. I was, to my great honor, elected president.

Unanimously.

Red Light, Yellow Light, Green Light

Way, way back in Chapter 1 we talked about self-esteem, and the 1-to-10 life score you give yourself. This is your invisible forehead number, which really isn't invisible. Others can always tell what it is, give or take a point. If you don't think much of yourself, it shows. Those who believe they're disguising low self-esteem kid themselves, nobody else.

We started with the number you give yourself, because that's where successful business communication and persuasion starts. If you're not telling yourself "Yes!" — ain't nobody else gonna tell you. We have here an immutable psychological law. If you're not reading 8 or 9 on your own gauges, you need a self-esteem tune-up, maybe an overhaul.

- Do it now.
- The book will be waiting for you, when you get back.

As I was saying, you begin by giving yourself a high forehead number, knowing full well that you deserve it. You can't stop here, though, because you really wear at least two numbers — the score you give yourself, and the score the world gives you. You're not going to win big in business persuasion unless both scores, yours and theirs, are high.

These scores, it turns out, are linked. One can drive the other down, but one can also lift the other.

NEER is primarily about the second life score, the one the world gives you. With NEER, you are always associated with people valued and esteemed by your buyers, so the buyers value and esteem you, from the moment you walk in and say Hi.

The fact that others automatically think more of you has a wonderful side-effect. It drives the score you give yourself higher. Rather than eroding your self-esteem, your day-to-day business builds it. With NEER, you ride an upward spiral. Up, my friends, is the only way to ride.

The old, cold call selling systems can drag you down. Cold prospects treat you coldly — who can blame them? — and you can't help but think less of yourself. It doesn't take long to knock points off your self-score. When your number starts sinking, buyers go from cold, to frigid, to downright frightful. Poor old Charlie started looking like a wreck, so people treated him like a wreck. Down and down he went until he was totaled.

Remember that there is more at stake here than feeling good about yourself, and having others like and respect you.

Persuasive success is at stake! Nothing less. A sale cannot, will not, happen if the buyer thinks less of you than he or she thinks of himself or herself. Nor can it happen if you think less of yourself than you think of the buyer. You must have, at least, mutually perceived **equality** to do good business.

In our seminars we illustrate this principle with traffic lights and acronyms. Naturally Existing Perceived Equality, **NEPE**, is the Yellow Light. The signal here is "Proceed With Caution." Nothing stops the sale from happening.

"Stop" is the unmistakable meaning of the Red Light, **N**aturally **E**xisting **P**erceived **I**nferiority, **NEPI**. The sale won't happen because either you, the buyer or, probably, both of you perceive you as **less-than** the buyer. You're stopped dead, and you're going to stay that way until the color changes.

You really want to see Green. This is **N**aturally **E**xisting **P**erceived **S**uperiority, **NEPS**, where you, the seller, have the psychological high ground, and are in a position to make things happen.

As in all aspects of human interaction, these concepts are subtle and multi-dimensional. The perceptions and what they signal operate only within the limits of your business relationship.

NEPS does **not** mean that you have to have a net worth of 8 figures to sell to the 7-figure folks. Nor does it mean that you must be a CEO to sell to the corporate vice-president. It couldn't mean that, or there wouldn't be much selling, would there?

Let's say you're a pavement contractor, approaching the wealthiest guy in the county, who has a driveway three miles long, which needs resurfacing something terrible. The man could buy you and sell you 20 times over. He plays tennis with the President,

N.E.P.I.   Red Light

Perceived
Inferiority

NO!

N.E.P.E.   Yellow Light

Perceived
Equality

MAYBE

N.E.P.S.   Green Light

Perceived
Superiority

YES!

for heaven's sake, and once had a barbecue for Lady Di.

Does all this mean you perceive him as your superior?

Absolutely not! Within the bounds of your relationship, it's you who have something he needs. He doesn't have a clue about driveways, but you are an expert. Your interest in his problem can help him. Within the relationship, you have a subtle psychological ascendancy.

Of course you must know you have it, not always easy when you're meeting a guy with three Lear jets. And he has to know it, by the way you handle yourself.

We're not talking about back-slapping or any sort of stupid, self-defeating over-familiarity, which doesn't work in Dogpatch, much less South Fork. The demeanor that works is self-assured, crisp, confident, down-to-earth and down-to-business. If you know why you're there, the prospect will know it.

Of course what gets you there, in the first place, is NEER. You couldn't be taking a meeting with this billionaire if somebody he knew and respected hadn't phoned or sent a note about you and your work. To meet the guy with the three-mile driveway, you approached through one of his neighbors for whom you've worked, whose mansion might be only a mile or two from the high-way. Otherwise, though, they're pretty much social equals. Maybe they've got some offshore joint ventures together, or sit on the same boards. It could be that their daughters have the same riding teacher and are going to Italy together next summer. Somehow or other, your prospect and whoever referred you have a NEER relationship that makes it natural and appropriate for the prospect to give you a listen.

NEER works just like this, in the real world. If your targets are up above treeline, you've got to stalk them at the same altitude, or pretty close to it. Our pavement contractor would have a hard time advancing, all at once, from doing work on $79,000 tract homes to the Driveways of the Rich and Famous.

Superman leaps tall buildings in a single bound. Mere mortals have to climb. NEER is more like an express elevator to the executive suites. Still, though, you have to make a stop or two on the way up. Otherwise you won't be expected, and welcomed, when you get to the penthouse.

Mama Was Wrong

I'm starting to worry about what kind of reception I'm going to get, Way Up Yonder. No, I'm not talking about the top floor of Big-DealCo's International Headquarters. I'm talking about the Afterlife, when I meet the folks who gave me the advice I'm now disputing. This book has been pretty hard on some of what the Old Folks said. A good deal of what they said was, indeed, The Wisdom Of The Ages. When they were wrong, though, they told us doozies.

If you grow up believing and trying to live by **everything** Mama told you, you're in deep trouble.

Case in point: All that stuff about being polite. She probably told you, the child, to tell adults "Yes Ma'am" and "Yes Sir" and be respectful, courteous and obedient.

On paper, this looks like better advice for an Irish setter than a human being! But isn't this what Mama told you? Some scolding and ear-twisting, and praise when you did everything right — and you probably **believed** what she told you.

Old beliefs, and old habits, die hard. Sometimes we need to put them out of their misery. This is particularly true here in The South, where politeness and reverence for the Old Folks are still very much admired. Grownups down here will, reflexively, call other grownups "Sir" and "Ma'am." It sounds very nice — I like hearing it myself. But it sends absolutely the wrong message if you're trying to do business on an equal footing. "Yes sir" sounds subservient, which is the last way you, the seller, want to sound. Always be respectful, but never subservient. Mr. Brown or Ms.

Smith sounds right, until you get to the first name basis. Even when you're completely comfortable, though, you shouldn't make the mistake of being flippant. Don't be servile — but don't presume on your relationships, either.

Personal power strikes early, quickly, and develops instant rapport. You'll know you've got it because you can feel it, and because of the way the other person treats you.

Remember this:

Perception isn't everything. But when you're selling, it might as well be!

CHAPTER 9

PARTNEER: Your First Board of Directors

THIS DOG *WILL* HUNT

Here in God's Country, if something is worn out or useless, we say "That old dog won't hunt."

The phrase means that the thing in question won't do what it's supposed to do. Maybe it used to, or maybe it never did. Either way, it's useless now, and you're better off without it.

My friend Randy Price, former president of Southwest Securities, who now lives in the Hill Country, is crazy about hunting and has champion hunting dogs. He tells me that the best dogs — the ones that **will** hunt — love it so much they're always doing it. If they're awake and outdoors, they're scenting and pointing. They hunt even when there's nothing to hunt. Birds aren't the point — hunting is. From the time they are puppies, champions show this winning drive.

Randy says the best people in his business have the same day-and-night devotion to their work. Champion investments people are always watching for new earnings opportunities and clients.

Successful persuaders in all fields have this 24-hour enthusiasm — I call it **achievement drive.**

Don't panic — I am **not** about to suggest that you sell day and night. If you do, you won't keep your friends for very long, your wife and kids either. Pretty soon your own Mama will stop letting you come over. She won't even return your phone calls!

I am, however, telling you to **prospect** all the time. Never cease to look for, and think about, ways to find new markets for your product, service or ideas.

A great seller doesn't need a college degree. But **CPA** is absolutely required. We're talking about the Hailey CPA:

Creative

Prospecting

Activity

This is what you must have, if you want championship selling success.

If you're awake and out of the house, you ought to be prospecting. You ought to be doing it because you love it, and because it's as natural as breathing.

Prospecting is, indeed, entirely natural. If you like other people and are curious about them — if not, why in the world are you selling? — it ought to be great fun to find out who's who and what's what, wherever you go. NEER research has something in common with everyday gossip and shoptalk, but it's really much more entertaining, because there's a point. Not only is there a point, there are rewards: More sales. More money. With NEER you grow your business and increase your earnings doing what you might be doing anyway — asking people questions about other people. You should always look for common ground, points of reference, link ups and hookups between you and those with whom you want to do business.

Whoa, some of you are saying, Hailey is telling me I have to work **after** I leave the office, and **before** I get there! This is, indeed, what I am telling you. If you've got a problem with it, you'd better be prepared to settle for mediocrity. But if mediocre isn't good enough, you must set yourself free of the 9-to-5, Monday–Friday routine, which doesn't allow nearly enough time and roaming room for extraordinary accomplishments.

Quit worryin' about quittin' time! As one friend of mine says, the 40-hour workweek is merely a foundation for high achievements. 9 to 5 gets you up to ground level. What you do from there on, is what the world can admire.

Atomic Theory of Business II

That ancient Greek who first said that the world is made of atoms had no idea what he was starting. In the last hundred years scientists have taken apart the atom and then busted the pieces into even smaller pieces. They're still finding little bits of this and that, and giving them weird names. But Atomic Theory, the grand pappy of all this scientific discovery, has held up just fine. A great theory always has room for unexpected guests.

Our Atomic Theory of Business is about to have an addition, a third kind of **fundamental unit**.

You'll remember that we started with the basic unit of NEER, the **N**, which is two people, one of them **selling**, and one of them **buying**. This **N** is the smallest and simplest Naturally Existing Economic Relationship.

From the point of view of you, the seller, it makes a lot of difference which side of the relationship — buyer or seller — you're on.

In an N_1, you're on the buyer's side.

N_1 Buyer's Side

Here you're either a customer of your prospect, or you have the endorsement of a customer. You are coming to the prospect from where the **money** comes. The implied relationship of you and that money gives the N_1 approach its automatic power. N_1 is the megawatt "Hello."

With N_2, you're on the seller's side.

N_2 Seller's Side

In the flow of money, N_2 goes upstream. Your influence is linked to the longstanding **trust** in the seller-to-buyer relationship. N_2 has less automatic, instant influence than N_1, and N_2 can feel a little riskier. Its ultimate power lies in developing a **Buyer For - Not Seller To** relationship for large clienteles, like my insurance company's customer base of retail grocers.

Put very simply,

- N_1 is where you start.
- N_2 is where you're going, if your goal is high-volume selling within established NEER systems.

Right now, you ought to be somewhere between your first N_1 NEER referral and a multi-million-dollar Buyer-For-Not-Seller-To marketing system. At this point, a new kind of NEER unit comes into play. This is the $\mathbf{P_N}$, the PARTNEER relationship.

PARTNEERSHIP
Noncompetitive sellers with shared clientele
pool what they know for their mutual benefit.

- Your first objective is **not** to sell to, or buy from, a PART-NEER.
- Both of you sell to the **same customers**.
- You are **not**, in any way, **competitors**.

PARTNEER stands for Professional Advisory Research Team (that) Networks Existing Economic Relationships. If this is too big of a mouthful, just remember Research Team.

The juice in a P_N is **information** and **power leads**. You and a PARTNEER each have knowledge that can help the other. You call on buyers that your PARTNEER wants to know about, and vice versa. Since you don't compete, it can't hurt either of you to share what you know — as long as each PARTNEER has integrity and value, and as long as you can **trust** each other.

An established PARTNEER relationship has something in common with N_1s and N_2s. Both **money** and **trust** bind PARTNEERs — money because you help each other make money, trust because this is the only basis for sharing vital information and valuable contacts.

P_Ns have another thing in common with N_1s and N_2s — these are sociable little units. They don't like to do things by themselves. Your first one-on-one PARTNEERship will naturally expand into a PARTNEER group, where a dozen or more non-competing peers, with a shared client base, meet on a regular basis to exchange information and leads.

PARTNEERing puts at your disposal the enormous power of the mutual support and combined creative energies of like-minded individuals. Every member of a 10-person group multiplies his or her prospecting reach. Suddenly you have 20 eyes, as many ears and 10 noses for sniffing out opportunities to expand your business. This sort of professional group synergy used to be the exclusive property of the rich and powerful. But with PARTNEERing you, whoever you are, can a have a seat on a **Board of Directors**. Since you're the founding member, you are **Chairman of the Board!**

As I look back, I realize I was using bits and pieces of NEER long before I started naming these the concepts and techniques, trying to understand them and, finally, teaching them.

In truth, I started thinking about teaching NEER to the public only about five years ago. Before that I said this stuff is too good to give away. I didn't want to train anybody but my own employees. But then I got to be 60 years old, and I felt like sharing what I had been jealously guarding.

With PARTNEER, I was practicing 40 years ago what I now preach, when I sold Light Crust Flour. I got together a group of a half-dozen people who sold things like aluminum foil, canned goods, evaporated milk, sugar and shortening.

Note, please, that these were **complementary** products, that went **with** my flour, not **against** it. I wouldn't have let the Pillsbury guy within a mile of my group.

Those fellows and I would get together regularly and jawbone about this manager and that store-owner, their likes and dislikes and peculiarities. There was always somebody in the group who wanted to get into a store that somebody else was already selling. We shared information about stores opening up and closing, new chains coming into our territories, which managers had been promoted or moved, and so on. Anything that anybody knew that could help somebody else's business was grist for our mill.

The shared information and insights made that group very valuable, but we made it better yet by pooling our selling efforts. Together we organized weekend store sales, with special displays and promotional pricing, that featured everybody's products. Each of us would be in a different supermarket on Friday night and Saturday, drumming up business for everybody else, so we each had six promotions going simultaneously.

Promoting our products jointly boosted sales. I did much better showing the folks everything they needed to make a peach cake, or chocolate-chip cookies, with all the ingredients at special prices, than I would have promoting Light Crust Flour, all by itself. Sometimes we'd have somebody passing out fresh-baked cookies or cake samples. I had a portable phonograph, and would play records by the Light Crust Dough Boys, my company's trademark country band. Between songs I'd announce drawings for prizes and 30-minute specials. Meanwhile, the other guys in the PARTNEER group were in other stores, working just as hard as I was. One year I worked 50 weekends. My reward for giving up Saturdays was shattering previous flour-selling records. I was promoted into sales management in record time and became one of the youngest managers in the industry's history.

We only did our extravaganzas for the leading supermarkets, which we called the Bell Cow stores. Then the other merchants would see what the big guys were doing, and follow their lead.

Why just **add**, when you can **multiply**? By marshalling the efforts of like-minded individuals, and applying those efforts where the selling leverage was greatest, we multiplied our results many times over.

PARTNEER marks an enormous forward step up your use of interpersonal power. So far, we've concentrated on your individual persuasive leverage, in one-on-one business relationships. Here you begin working within a group. This takes you into the realm of the Master Mind principle, which I first learned reading Napoleon Hill's *Think And Grow Rich*, the motivational book that changed my life. Hill taught that two or more minds, joined together in harmony, working together toward a major purpose, create a third, extremely powerful mind, the Master Mind, which is greater than the sum of its parts. On paper this can sound a little overblown, maybe even spooky. But try it just once, and get the Master Mind on your side, and you'll never doubt it again.

Star Search

Groups are as fragile as they are powerful. Whoever said "One bad apple spoils the bunch" was not talking about Golden Delicious and Jonathan. The subject was people, and the amazing ability of one jerk to ruin everything for everybody else. Judas showed the power of the rat-factor back in biblical times.

Yes, one little old **turkey** can disrupt a Gathering Of Eagles, so the eagles go off in a huff and never want to gather again. This is another one of those human oddities. Maybe someday we'll be able to ask God how come we're built like this. In the mean time, we just have to accept it and work it to our advantage.

Pick your PARTNEERs very carefully. This is particularly true of the first one, who will co-found your group. The group will live and die by the professionalism and stability of the founders and the first person or two they pick.

You're looking for a go-getter with the same target market, who is not a competitor. If you sell auto insurance, this might be the top salesperson at a certain car dealership. If you sell office paper products, it might be the best copier seller in the area. If your game is steel and aluminum, maybe it's the number one welding supply salesman.

Aim high in your search. A so-so PARTNEER may not put enough effort into it. Even if she or he does try hard, the input will be only mediocre.

Always pick **all** of your associates carefully. Your results will rise, or sink, to the level of those with whom you surround yourself. This is another one of those immutable, mysterious human laws.

You don't need to know exactly who you're looking for, to start looking. Keep your eyes and ears open when you're out on calls, ask a few questions, and you will, most likely, pick up the trail of a seller who is running way ahead of the pack. The evidence might be the predominance of a certain brand — one company's copiers, computers, kitchen equipment or pretzels and chips. When you see a certain brand is ahead of the others, ask one of your customers, Who **is** this hotshot, who's moving all of this product?

Start asking your customers to name the best seller — other than yourself, of course — who calls on them. Nine times out of ten, you'll start hearing one name over and over. Business worlds are small, and people know who the stars are.

You can find the leaders at auto dealerships by looking at awards and plaques on the wall. Your PARTNEER-to-be might be employee-of-the-month, or seller-of-the-year. Watch the local newspapers to see who's winning Caribbean cruises and other incentive awards. You can call a given company and ask for the name of its top-producing seller. Conspicuous success is usually, just like it says, conspicuous. People have no reason to hide it.

Pick person over brand. You're linking up with a fellow persuader, not what is being sold. Don't be dazzled by some new make or model, which is taking the world by storm. Your star is the persuader, not the product.

The best approach to a prospective PARTNEER is NEER-style. Have a customer shared by you and your candidate call and make a brief introduction. All that needs to be said is that the customer recommended the candidate to you, and that you are forming a group of the area's top sellers. Any gung-ho seller will want to know more.

When you call, say who you are and why you selected this particular seller — everybody's raving about the job he or she does, etc. — and propose a very short breakfast meeting. (You might want to refer back to **Hailey's Good Morning Special** back in the chapter on 7 to 1, which tells how to do business at breakfast.)

There are two purposes to this first meeting.

• First, to make sure that you want to PARTNEER with this seller.

• Second, to explain the concept and get a commitment to found a PARTNEERship and make it work.

Remember that you have no obligation to include this person, if you don't want to. Chances are you will. After your research, there shouldn't be unpleasant surprises. But maybe you just don't click, or you find out something that rules this person out. If there's a problem, face it now. Momentary awkwardness with a stranger is better than starting a group doomed to die a slow death. By then your first pick won't be a stranger, but an **enemy.**

Five qualities of a good PARTNEER:

- A good performer. Your selling results will tend to match your PARTNEERs'.

- High Integrity. Trusted and liked by clientele and community.

- Goals and values are in-sync with yours. Look at where this person's been, where he or she is going. Your outlook and aspirations should be compatible.

- What he or she does is relevant. This person can really help you.

- Your contributions can be as good as your PARTNEER's.

If your reading on all five points is positive, you've got a match. Congratulations! You have just doubled your intelligence-gathering, prospecting reach. You've also got somebody on your side. Business, with the help of your new PARTNEERship, will be better and more fun.

The first order of business, once you have good rapport and trust, is to add another member, who will complement the duo. When the trio is in harmony, make it a quartet. Never force new members on yourselves, or grow for the sake of growing. Make your selections with the greatest care. The first four members will make you or break you. Later on, a bad apple can be disposed of, but a bad member in the group's nucleus can ruin the whole group.

Signs Of A Bad PARTNEER:

- Taker, not a giver. Unwilling to share his or her intelligence. Won't get truly interested in other members' problems.

- Untrustworthy. Violates confidentiality of group, deliberately misleads others.

- No commitment. Can't be relied on to come to get-togethers. Arrives late, if at all, won't take things seriously.

• Motormouth. Talks more, says less. Uncontrolled, Mr. or Ms. Flapjaw is death on any group.

• Doesn't get it. This should be considered an **early warning sign**. If somebody says "That's nice, but what good can it do for me?" you probably don't want him in the group.

Be alert for the positive signs, too. The most important sign is that you and every member of the group are comfortable with each new member. Rapport is critical — you must like and enjoy each other. One member's discomfort should be enough to eliminate a candidate. Most of the time you'll know right off when you've got a keeper, because you'll **feel** it. He or she will know it and feel it, too. The people you're looking for are looking for you, every time. It feels great to find each other.

Hailey's Rules Of Order

As the group grows, it becomes necessary to keep order and maintain the group's focus. You, the founder, are by default the leader, in function if not in name. It isn't really necessary to name officers, as long as somebody — probably you — keeps the group in control, and focused on the business at hand, which is sharing information and leads. A little bit of drifting and time-wasting, and you'll quickly lose the most worthwhile members of your group.

The first bit of organizing is scheduling your meetings, which should be once a week, and no longer than about 50 minutes. Set times for meetings to end. And end on time, without fail, so others can schedule their activities around meetings and avoid wasting time. Don't even try to do your PARTNEERing after work, over cocktails. A social hour will be social, nothing else. Meet at the start of the day, early enough that you're not taking anything out of anybody's day. Find a restaurant with a table big enough for your group, in a private, quiet corner or, better yet, a separate room. Restaurant owners will probably be very accommodating, at this hour.

Strict parliamentary procedure is not necessary, unless that sort of thing turns the group on. But you want to stick to a regular format.

Each member of the group has the floor for about five minutes. First he or she briefly summarizes the past week, customers called, sales made, what was done and what this seller wants to do, along with any observations of particular interest to group members. After the summary statement, the group can pose questions or contribute information. The style here is casual and the pace quick. Keep things moving, so everybody gets his or her five minutes, and everybody gets something of value at each meeting.

PARTNEER sound bites:

Joe Postage Meter: That old copier at Ace Title Company is dyin', Myra. Maybe you ought to give Robin the office manager a call. Get with me after the meeting, and I'll tell you what I know.

Anne Marie Accountant: I was just up at Brown, Brown and Brown and they are expanding. They opened up a whole new floor, and they're hiring new staff.

Orville Office Supplies: What is with those creeps in Purchasing at Technico? Can anybody here tell me what I need to do, to get through the door?

Laureen Lawyer: I just heard that PeachTree Group, out of Atlanta, is looking at the old doorknob factory. They want to do shops and galleries on the first floor, and loft-style condos upstairs. There's going to be a health club, and everything.

Before long, it becomes second nature to keep a lookout for your PARTNEER friends, while they're looking out for you. What you learn is only the beginning of PARTNEERing's benefits. As the group gels, there's a sense that you all belong to a team, with everybody supporting everybody else, cheering each other's victories, helping when help is needed. Not only is business better, it's more fun, and less lonely. PARTNEER takes another big bite out of FEAR.

Hang on a minute — I believe I'm picking up another objection: "Come on Hailey, you're not tellin' me anything new. This is **Networking**, and it's old as the hills."

Wrong.

If this is networking, I am King Juan Carlos, and my dog Precious is an Arabian horse. Networking, as anybody knows who has tried it, is where you breathe heavily and exchange business cards. Networking only keeps people's interest until there's no more wine and hors d'oeuvres. PARTNEERing is entirely focused and results-oriented. This represents a quantum-level improvement on meeting and greeting. After all, nobody is going to share really vital information, or — especially — good prospects, with people met on a catch-as-catch-can basis. Networking isn't sufficiently deep, formal or **trusting**. If you find a Networking group that works, it's probably really a PARTNEER group, but the members don't know the name. Join it.

Back to the PARTNEER meetings:

They may be as formal, or as informal, as the group likes, so long as they get the job done. Remember to keep the focus on positive **results**, not the process. One option is come to each meeting with lead information cards, with the basics of potential buyers, and a line or two of facts or hunches to help others make an approach and a sale. It works, too, to begin or end the meeting with a five-minute presentation by a member about something worthwhile he or she read, learned at a seminar, or picked up at work. Presentation-givers rotate through the entire membership — nobody has the option of **not** speaking.

Set and keep high standards. As the group grows beyond its original nucleus, application for membership should be formalized. Let each prospective PARTNEER attend one meeting. At the next meeting, members can talk over the new addition and vote. Require more than a simple majority for approval. You might consider giving each member veto power over new additions. A few bad vibes between individuals, and group harmony will suffer. If you don't have harmony and trust, you don't have PARTNEER. Pickiness, and making candidates wait a couple weeks to find out if they're in, won't hurt the group's image at all. If people believe they're getting into the winner's circle, they'll try harder to be winners. You'll also want a procedure to drop losers, which you should do without hesitation. Your PARTNEER group is not a social club, and you have no obligation to those who don't contribute.

Much as you want to be persnickety about people, loosen up when you think about professions. The more creative the mix, the more exciting the results. Your best PARTNEERs often are not immediately obvious. Those whose clients wear customer-tailored silk suits would probably profit by exchanging information with the person who sells those suits. The best hairdresser and dressmaker in town knows who's who, and what's what, among the leading ladies. The manager of the most exclusive downtown club is undoubtedly a fount of inside information. Whoever makes signs and billboards often knows, before anybody else, which companies are about to move, or start a big campaign. Commercial realtors have all sorts of information about noteworthy comings and goings. And, of course, there are the more obvious synergies — CPAs and investments brokers, real estate agents and those who write homeowners insurance, lawyers and just about anybody.

A top Dallas residential realtor who went through our seminar has put together a **huge** PARTNEER group, with about 30 people. The members are those most-sought by new arrivals in town— painters, landscapers, insurance agents, barbers and hairdressers, even a massage therapist. She prints a list which she hands out to her home-buyers. In return, she gets wonderful information about who's coming and who's going from the business people on her list. Everybody involved is flattered, happy, and benefiting from the arrangement!

P.A.R.T.N.E.E.R.

Look for professionals with your target market who are not competitors. Use your imagination.

1.	Computer Sales	32.	Association Executive
2.	Attorney	33.	Business Writer
3.	CPA	34.	L.B.O. Specialist
4.	Commercial Insurance	35.	Venture Capital
5.	Stock Broker	36.	Airplane Sales
6.	Business Broker	37.	Decorator
7.	Business Consultant	38.	Office Supply
8.	M. D.	39.	Club Manager
9.	Dentist	40.	Accounts Payable
10.	Chamber of Commerce Manager	41.	Convention Planner
11.	Industry Development Bd.	42.	Convention Bureau
12.	Employment Agency	43.	Board Member
13.	Head Hunter	44.	Architect
14.	Luxury Car Sales	45.	Airline Sales
15.	Travel Company	46.	Consultant
16.	Audio Visual Sales	47.	Political
17.	Magazine	48.	Clergy
18.	Newspaper	49.	Charitable Foundations
19.	Radio	50.	Social Leader
20.	Advertising Agency	51.	Home Builder
21.	Hotels	52.	Personal Service
22.	Real Estate - Residential	53.	Sports Personality
23.	Real Estate - Commercial	54.	Veterinarian
24.	Men's Clothing Sales	55.	Human Resource People
25.	Women's Clothing Sales	56.	Celebrity
26.	Banker	57.	Sales Manager
27.	Financial Planner	58.	Sales and Marketing Clubs
28.	Savings and Loan	59.	Life Insurance
29.	Time Management Systems	60.	Engineer
30.	Business Incentives	61.	Jeweler
31.	Business Professor	62.	Signmaker

ACTION PLAN

PARTNEERing

High time to get off our whatsits and down to business. It's been way too long since we had an Action Plan.

The goal here is to put into practice what you just read, by forming your own PARTNEER group. Necessary instructions are all in this chapter. If it isn't immediately clear where you ought to be seeking your first PARTNEER, take a look at the list on page 210.

• Choose members with greatest care. Everybody must be comfortable with everybody else.

• Keep meetings brief and to-the-point. Be casual, but stick to business.

• Keep simple notes of meetings. Always watch for potential problems and ways to improve.

• Immediately vote out anybody who **betrays** the integrity and harmonious feelings of the group. **NO EXCEPTIONS!**

• Remember that PARTNEER is a bank of information and support. If withdrawals exceed deposits, the bank will close forever.

CHAPTER 10

Where NEER™ Will Take You

HAILEY'S PYRAMID

Tell me, right this minute, the names of the Kings that the Great Pyramids of Giza were built for?

Can't answer, can you?

The Pyramids teach a valuable lesson: Building big and fancy for after you're dead, so nobody will forget you, is a terrible investment.

Old Pharaoh should have invested in life, like Moses or Jesus or Buddha. They had small tombstones, but **huge** ideas, and their names are being spoken by millions, while you read this page.

As my friend the Rev. Buckner Fanning, the well-known minister and biblical scholar, points out, a lot more people name their sons Paul and their dogs Pharaoh, than vice versa.

One of those old-time Egyptian pyramids, big on the bottom and small on the top, looks to me like Discouragement set in stone. Think what it would be like to build one of those dudes! Back-strain and blisters aside, you've always got diminishing returns.

Going up, layer by layer, a pyramid gets smaller. Every time you take a step up, there's less room. Eventually, at its highest point, there's nothing to the pyramid but a single, solitary stone.

What happens when you want to add a level or two? **Nothing** happens, because you can't build on top of that stone.

I don't mean to criticize — but Old Pharaoh was building 'em **upside down!**

One stone sounds more like a beginning than an end, doesn't it? And shouldn't the top floor be biggest, so the higher you go, the more room you have? And why would anybody give up the option to grow upward?

We here at Planned Marketing Associates have redesigned the pyramid. With a couple minor alterations, Pharaoh's billion-pound tombstone becomes an inspiration for living and a model for achievement.

Put the small part on the bottom, the big part on top, and you've got something to stand back and admire. The higher it goes, the more it grows. Not too far up, and the top floor has room for a domed stadium. Build it higher and the penthouse is as big as the State of Arkansas!

An architect friend of mine says we need to put in a disclaimer here: Hailey's Pyramid is an impossibility, from the engineering standpoint, even if you build it with stainless steel and plexiglas.

That's OK, though, because we build with **mind**, **spirit**, **person-to-person trust** and **respect** and **loyalty**, the **exchange of wealth**, and **wealth itself**. We measure height in terms of **self-actualization** and one's own feeling of **success**, and calculate floor space by potentialities, **satisfaction** and **financial reward!** Building like this, the **NEER** way, construction is limited only by imagination and commitment to succeed. Remove the limiting beliefs and thoughts, and there are no limits.

Take a look at the pyramid, and see if you can tell where you

HAILEY'S N. E. E. R. PYRAMID

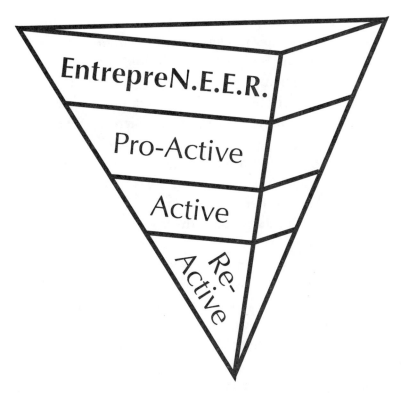

With each step up, your satisfaction, potential and financial rewards **soar!**

are right now. If you've been keeping up with the lessons in this book, you ought to be up where the view is terrific, with enough floor space for indoor soccer. The information you've gotten so far should take you at least 80 percent of the way to the top of your field. This is where you want to be, among the 20 percent who enjoy at least 80 percent of the successes and financial rewards.

So who are those people down at ground-level, looking about as big as ants? You can tell they're not ants, though, because they're not running around, making themselves useful. They just sit there.

Those little specks are the rock-bottom **reactive** sellers. They don't move because they're waiting for the phone to ring or somebody to come through the door. They hold still until somebody calls or walks in. Then they keep holding still until the poor customer **demands** some kind of attention. But then the customer better know what he wants, because the inactive seller's product knowledge is on a par with his or her energy-level.

Really **re**active sellers are the stones around modern retailers' necks. They account, in large part, for the recent resurgence in catalog shopping. Mail order is impersonal, but it's better than being ignored and insulted in person, which is exactly what happens at all too many businesses.

This is no way to sell, and no way to make a living.

The first stone of our sales pyramid belongs to the higher echelons of **reactive** sellers. These people know their products, and are terrific spielers. Set a customer loose in their midst and they **pounce**. They'll do anything, short of violence, to get to a customer before other sellers.

But, with no buyers in sight, these **re**active sellers look a good deal like their **in**active counterparts. They sit and wait. What are they waiting for? For the big signs on the showroom windows, TV ads, factory incentives, rebates, special financing — and whatever else the marketing department has dreamed up — to catch the buyers' attention and bring them in. We call these sellers reactive because they're only equipped to **re**act, and rely totally on others to bring in the customers.

There are **re**active sellers as close as your nearest auto show-room, waiting for the dealership's "spray and pray" marketing techniques to send them an "up."

And how are things down in **Re**active-ville?

Not too good.

Things are better in the next layers on our selling pyramid, which belong to sellers who rely on traditional, **active** prospecting techniques. These people have gotten off their hind-ends, and off the ground. They go out and seek what the lower-level sellers sit and wait for — buyers — using such time-honored techniques as cold calling and telemarketing. Active sellers make more money than their inactive and reactive counterparts — and they **earn** it. Success at this level requires enormous discipline and emotional fortitude. Repeated cold calling is one of the toughest jobs in the world.

Higher-level active sales people get extensive product training, work on their communication and influencing skills, move into referral selling, and begin targeting markets, as well as individual prospects. The more astute active sellers move from transaction selling to **solution** selling, developing a growing sensitivity to buyers' individual needs. Still, though, improving one's productive results is largely a matter of **more** contacts with buyers, rather than **better** contacts. The traditional techniques and philosophies emphasize numbers: Sell more by calling more. They improve the **score**, but do absolutely nothing about the **odds**. Results, at the very best, might be 1 in 10. One buyer out of every 10 says Yes. The ratio is 1 in 10 if you call on 2 people a day, and 1 in 10 if you call on 25.

There's very little control here over the seller-buyer relationship. Things happen. But you are powerless to **make** them happen. Traditional techniques are all limited by the **law of averages**.

Extraordinarily talented individuals can, and do, make very

good livings with traditional cold calling techniques. Still,though, it is difficult for the most of us to get much beyond OK. The cost of excellence, without NEER's persuasive leverage, is just too high.

I'd guess that you were somewhere in the traditional, active ranks when you bought this book. You were adept at a few of the more sophisticated "old school techniques," doing OK, but wanting more, and not knowing how to get it.

OK and traditional techniques end at the same place — which is the place where **pro**activity begins. NEER takes you over this all-important threshold. Learn this system, believe in it, and practice it, and you'll empower yourself to make things happen. And never again will your movements in the business world be random. Your income will rise, as your stress levels fall.

Part I of this book, **Programming The Two-Billion-Dollar Computer** was all about taking the **random** out of your marketing **motion**. 80/20, **7 to 1** and the **15 System** are analytical tools for making clear, do-able decisions about **who** you ought to be calling on, **what** you ought to do when you call, **where** and **when** and **how** many times. Together these three techniques are a master system for analyzing and organizing your selling efforts.

Part 2 is about a new kind of power — **NEER Power** — that brings unprecedented control over your business relationships. With NEER you can, literally, **make** things happen. You can make the most sought-after buyers receive you and listen with respect. By forging chains of buyer-seller links, you can approach any prospect from a position of dignity and respect and influence. As you gain power, all the emotional hazards of selling lose power, so there's very little left to be afraid of. This journey **From Fear To NEER** is one of the most exhilarating trips you can take. What you've learned so far is enough to make selling a much happier and more rewarding occupation, and earn you lifetime membership in Walter Hailey's 80/20 Club, among the top 20 percent, who do four-fifths of the world's selling business.

You're now better off than you were, but you don't want to stop here. NEER itself doesn't want to stop here. The System's natural tendency is to soar ever higher and wider, just like our redesigned, right side-up pyramid. Once you're using NEER, the system wants to carry you upward. Our next step up takes us over another important threshold. Here you can make a quantum leap, multiplying results by working with many buyers within established economic systems. This, in a sense, is NEER's Destiny, where it will take you if you give it a chance.

We call this next level **EntrepreNEERing**. You are, in effect, starting your own business, in a new place, which is all yours. This doesn't mean quitting your current job. It does mean, though, that you're taking control of your own destiny in business, putting all your experience and skills and imagination to work to bring the power of **groups** of buyers into play. The seller who controls the markets runs the show!

E Pluribus Unum

A few billion years ago, the most advanced life-forms were single cells swimming around in seawater. One-celled life was an incredible advance over no life at all. But incredible wasn't good enough. The cells started affiliating, living in groups and specializing, in order to be more efficient and competitive. The groups got bigger, more mobile and smarter, becoming — among other things — **Us!**

You and I are walking, talking biological NEERs, grand strategic alliances of cells that work to protect each other's interests.

Your NEER relationships will tend to evolve the same way as life did, from the small and simple to the large and complex. Sooner or later your individual contacts begin to group and organize into economic systems. The systems, which are made up of individuals, function as **wholes**, and confer all sorts of competitive advantages on those who belong to them. There's a world of difference between being an **insider** and an **outsider**, when you're trying to do business within one of these economic systems.

The inevitable direction of NEER is **in**, toward insider relations with buyers who belong to large seller-buyer systems. The system carries you from the Wide World of Anybody to lucrative **niche markets,** and closer ties with buyers, until you're perceived as one of them — **buying for** — **not selling to** your targeted clientele.

My own best NEER, the deal for selling insurance to grocers through grocery warehouses, took my company — literally — inside the system. Our offices were in the warehouses. The customers were billed for their monthly premiums along with their carrots and peas and ice cream. By becoming part of the familiar, trusted day-to-day flow of business — which had been there a hundred years before Smiling Walter showed up — we virtually eliminated psychological **resistance** on the part of our buyers.

When you work within an existing system, as part of the system, it is at least 82 percent easier for the buyer to tell you Yes! Unfamiliarity, in selling, equals resistance. It is always easier to persuade people to do a little more of what they're already doing, than to get them to do something entirely new.

On the other side of our persuasive coin were the unique advantages we could offer. First, by cultivating the niche market, we developed specialized expertise. We spoke the customers' language and understood their special needs, better than our competitors possibly could. This unique understanding, alone, gave us a leg up. We became absolutely invincible by adding value and tailoring products for our clients.

The amazing thing was that nobody gave us a fight! At first, they didn't even notice us. The world saw our clientele as small potatoes — who cares about the corner grocery store? From the warehouse side, we saw 100,000 affiliated grocers and billions in business. By the time other insurance agencies saw what we were up to, they were too late! Our lead was established. And NEER was working for us.

Once we were up and running, success was almost too easy. The competition let us take all that business, without a fight. And the grocers said Yes! to our program more than 8 out of 10 times. This was an **800 percent** improvement on the previous closing ratio — which wasn't all that bad, even before NEER. We paid lower commissions and provided very small offices, but the best people in the business came to work for us because they could make more money, with none of the combative atmosphere and repeated rejection that normally is part of selling insurance. We wouldn't even let our people take clients out to lunch! Neither the sellers nor the clients minded, though, because our business was so good for everybody. Everybody either made more money, or saved more money, than they had before. We were a team.

What's that you say?

"Come on Hailey, what does this have to do with me? I don't have a snowball's chance in Hades of getting into anybody's warehouse to sell my stuff to any mass clientele. The picture you paint is gorgeous, but I ain't in it!"

You **are** in it, whoever you are.

You are in it because you don't need an entire beginning-to-end distribution system to make NEER work. It works in pieces. Virtually any sort of economic system can be put to work for you.

Sometimes getting **inside** the system is as simple as signing up and paying dues.

One of our seminar participants, who deals in insurance and financial instruments, approached one of his state's medical professional associations, to see about getting the group's official endorsement for his products. The answer, not too surprisingly, was No.

Other agents and brokers had made the same approach, gotten the same No, and moved on. Our man didn't move on, though. He found out that vendors and suppliers could get special membership in the association. He joined, and immediately began to differentiate himself from other supplier members, who did little more than take out ads in the association publications and set up booths and hospitality suites at the annual meetings. Our seller sponsored golf tournaments and special seminars. His extraordinary efforts on behalf of the membership did not go unnoticed. He quickly became one of the family, winning the business of one-third of those doctors in **one year**. He will, most likely, have two-thirds before another year is out. Not only is he selling big to his targeted client base, the association recently gave him its endorsement. He is now an officially designated preferred supplier — exactly what he wanted to be, in the first place!

Romancing those doctors was neither cheap nor easy, but this seller has been repaid, many times over, by lucrative new business.

NEER works beautifully for our seller without the benefits of economies of scale, or specially tailored products. He sells standard policies and financial instruments, the same offered by agents all over the country. He succeeds because of the power of **niche marketing**, and being a recognized specialist in serving the needs of one branch of medical professionals. The doctors also benefit from this deepening relationship. Instead of dealing with generalists, they have a bonafide expert in their needs, who speaks their language. The official endorsement of the association, by the time our seller got it, was richly deserved. The association was doing itself and its membership a favor.

Besides the tangible benefits he could offer, our seller's approach to many practitioners put the psychological power of the group on his side. It is much, much easier to persuade someone to do what his or her peers are already doing. One of the greatest obstacles to "Yes, I'll take it!" is the buyer's fear of being wrong, and looking foolish in others' eyes. Knowing that peers have said Yes! does away with this fear. The group's agreement that your program is worth buying validates the decision for the hesitant.

Some people say niche like "neesh," because it is originally from the French, and that's how they say it in Paree. But we sellers ought to say **niche** so it rhymes with **rich**. The two words go together. Niche marketing, when you get it working for you, can make you rich. So can selling to groups, getting inside an existing mass affiliation or distribution, or developing a strategic alliance system and using it to reach and influence a large client base. Affiliate and associate and let the pre-existing organizations and systems help you sell.

Jingle the change in your pocket or purse and think about what's written on every one of the coins. E Pluribus Unum — From Many, One. There is strength in numbers.

ACTION PLAN

Which Floor Are You On?

We at Planned Marketing are all for the recent emphasis on goal-setting. You've got to be going **somewhere** to get **anywhere!** This is true even if you have to change destinations in mid-trip. Columbus knew exactly where he was going when he discovered America — he was going to China. Without that end firmly in mind, he would have turned back in mid-ocean.

But, just as important as where you're going, is your point of departure. You must know where you are now. Otherwise you can't make good plans for getting to your destination.

• Turn back to the illustration of Hailey's Persuasion Pyramid and study it.

• Which level are you on, right now?_____

• How long have you been on it?_____

• Is this too long?_____

• What is your short-term plan to rise to the next level? Be specific — say what you intend to do, with whom and when.

_____

_____

_____

_____

_____

_____

• Don't just daydream about it— do it!
• Which level is your ultimate goal?_____
• When do you want to get there?_____

Don't worry about the plan, just yet. You'll be much more ready to plan after you read the next, and final, chapters of this book.

❖ ❖ ❖

CHAPTER 11

LQ & IQ: The Big Picture

PROSPECTING FOR IDEAS AND LEVERAGE

The selling you do next will be a product of your own intelligence, and nobody else's. We're now beyond the ABCs of NEER, which can be taught alphabetically, one after the other. How you put together these basic moves will be your decision. Each unique combination of persuader, product and clientele dictates a unique NEER solution.

You can be sure, though, that there **is** a solution. Somewhere, somehow your current business relationships can be expanded into large-scale success, using basic NEER techniques, duplicating what works until you've built a great big Marketing Machine. No matter how small your current business, it can lead to something big.

It's time to begin a new kind of prospecting. Up to this point we've concentrated on prospecting for people — your ideal clients and the intermediary contacts who can lead you to them.

Now we're going to raise our sights and start prospecting for **ideas**. The key to your biggest NEER successes is an idea, which is already in your head and in the world around you. It's there in pieces. You have to put them together. Creativity is really about combining existing Truths in new ways — so they're Truer than they ever were before. The Truths you need are close at hand. By linking these together you can increase your **IQ — Idea Quotient** — with new concepts and plans to open the doors you need to open, and add value to what you sell, to the point that telling you "Yes!" is the best decision your buyer can possibly make.

IQ is, however, only Stage One of the NEER Creative Process. The greatest selling idea in the world won't come to much, if you don't know **where** to put the idea to work for you. Ideas must be used where they have the maximum amount of leverage. We call this principle **LQ — Leverage Quotient**. LQ and IQ must always work together.

LQ is where you are in a NEER economic system. A good idea in a bad place might as well be a bad idea.

Think about what might have happened if I tried to apply my own bright idea — mass marketing insurance to retail grocers — at some other point in the grower-to-grocer chain.

Maybe I could have worked through the outfit up in Ohio that supplies most of the nation's radishes. (There really is such a company, with a near-monopoly on radishes.) Draw it out on paper, and you'll see that hundreds of thousands of food retailers are, indeed, customers of that one company. There are, in fact, a lot more retail radish customers than customers of any single food wholesaler.

But radishes are too close to the ground, and too far from the customers. This is not a natural leverage-point, as a wholesale house is. Selling insurance to grocery stores — if you tried to do it with radishes — would be unworkable, if not dumb.

LQ within a NEER system is every bit as important as location to a store- or restaurant-owner. Business owners like to say that location is **everything**. It's really only half of everything. The idea — the right kind of business — is the other half.

Your Big Idea

Why create mediocrity, when you can copy genius?

The question expresses a rock-bottom principle of what we teach here at Planned Marketing Associates: Build on other people's accomplishments. Copy what works.

Most of the best creative ideas in the world are 10 percent improvements on proven concepts. This is true, in spades, in marketing and sales. When you hunt for your own big opportunities, look at the people who are already successful, and how they succeed.

- **Emulate** the winners.
- **Replicate** systems that work.
- **Duplicate** successes!

Spend less time trying to be brilliant, and more time studying and imitating what the brilliant have done, and are doing. Adapt somebody else's brilliant solutions to your own needs, and your results will be just as brilliant as theirs. When you start emulating, replicating and duplicating, remember to reproduce each step of their actions carefully, A to Z. If you leave something out, it's apt to be what makes the whole business **work**.

There's no disgrace at all to driving a **used** idea, when you're on your way to the bank! Unlike cars, ideas get shinier and better-looking and faster every time somebody else takes possession. If an idea is useful today, it's **new**.

The ideas to look for, in selling, belong to two basic categories:
• Door-Openers
• Value-Adders

Door-Openers catch the customers' attention, giving them a reason to want to get next to you, which may or may not be directly related to what you're selling. **Value-Adders** make what you're selling a better deal for the buyer. Add enough value, and saying Yes! becomes irresistible. **Door-Openers** are your **Hi!** ideas, for getting in the door. **Value-Adders** are your **Buy!** ideas, which give customers an irresistable reason to tell you **Yes!**

Big Names, Bigger Sales

1) Celebrity Selling

My own best Door-Openers were **celebrities**. I called my big-name influencers **face cards**. Whenever I could, I worked along-side people who were famous and well-liked among our buyers. One of them was Bud Wilkinson, the legendary Oklahoma football coach. Business people came to meetings with us just because they were dying to meet Bud To meet him, though, they had to learn about our insurance company. Would the name Walter Hailey, and Total Insurance Planning, have gotten them to sit down with us? Maybe, maybe not. But this college-sports hero took all the maybe out of it.

What Bud was to football, Stuart Hunt and John D. Murchison were to big business and big money. After those two Dallas-based magnates became involved in our insurance deal, they'd come to grocers' conventions. Customers who might otherwise have passed us by stopped at our booth and came to our meetings, for the privilege of meeting them. Their names were just as big a draw on Wall Street, after our company went public.

Of course Coach Wilkinson and Stuart Hunt and John Murchison were not just hanging around because they liked attention, or because they wanted to be nice to their good friend Walter Hailey. They were always much more than mere figureheads, participating in our businesses as partners, investors, stockholders and board members.

Value is always part of selling with celebrities. First, the value of what you offer must more than equal the celebrity's investment of time and energy. And value must be good for the buying public. Otherwise, both sales and the celebrity's image will suffer. If Michael Jordan put his face and autograph on boxes of bad, over-priced breakfast cereal, he'd do himself a lot more harm than he'd do the cereal company good.

There must be a fit between you, what you have to offer, and the person whose name and fame you want to use. Guest appearances by Garth Brooks and Cher would do wonders for the traffic at anybody's grand opening — but few businesses can afford them. Until you can, you'll have to content yourself with people at your own level, to whom you can offer attractive incentives. You might consider putting the best-known local high school coach on the payroll, as a part-time seller. He or she probably needs the money as much as you need the coach's name and presence. Anybody who draws the right kind of attention and credibility to you and your product, for whom you can make association with you worthwhile, is a potential celebrity seller.

2) Raising Your Own Profile

It helps, too, to raise your own profile, by becoming an active member of fraternal organizations, civic groups, charities, even holding political office. Increasing your own stature and name-recognition can increase your persuasive leverage with buyers. You can't sell people until you **meet** them. And you'll meet a whole lot more people when you become somebody **they** want to meet.

Take every opportunity for **public speaking** that comes your way. This has a powerful dual benefit: First, it makes your name and face better-known in the community. Second, it hones the communication skills that you need in selling. Once you're comfortable speaking to 100 people, you won't be scared of talking with one person! And the more you speak, the more effective your speaking becomes.

Around Dallas, I got an enormous amount of exposure emceeing events, warming up the crowds and introducing the featured speakers. A good emcee, it turns out, is harder to find than a featured speaker. And emcees get a lot more work. An appearance or two a year, as featured speaker, is all I could have hoped for. But I could emcee, all over town, all the time! The more I emceed, the more people asked each other that wonderful question — Who **is** that little guy? — and the closer I came to meeting them and doing business with them.

I used to be **terrified** of getting up in front of people. One of my earliest and best mentors, John Hicks, my boss at Burrus Mills, cured me of crowd-phobia, once and for all. He did it by making me emcee of the company's trademark country band, the Light Crust Dough Boys, which had its own radio show and is still very well-known in this part of the country. One of Texas' governors, W. Lee "Pappy" O'Daniel, first got into the public eye emceeing the band, as I later did. Dough Boy albums include Country Music immortals Bob Wills, Leo McAuliffe and Hank Thompson.

At first I found the public eye more than a little unnerving. After some particularly sorry emceeing, Marv "Smoky" Montgomery, the Dough Boys' banjo player, helped me out. He came up after the show with this friendly advice: "Walter, if that ever happens again, I won't get mad at you. I'm gonna **kill** you." Did I start doing better?

You tell me.

3) Event Selling
With the Dough Boys, I learned about the power of **event sell-**

ing, which is a second cousin of celebrity selling. The right kind of event can get people together, and put them in a buying mood. The weekend shindigs my PARTNEERs and I put on in supermarkets were very effective small-scale selling events. At many of the band's appearances, at fairs and evening shows, the crowds couldn't buy flour, because it wasn't for sale. We were, nevertheless, **selling** it, and the people would, sooner or later, **buy** it, because of the Dough Boys' good country music.

• **Warning!** Do not get carried away with the idea of exposure.

Always keep in mind what the word means: It can, if you use it right, help you **sell**. But if you're not careful, you can also **die** of it, or **be arrested** for it. If you seek exposure for its own sake, you're wasting money and time. Raise your profile only if you've got solid reason to believe it will raise your profits.

4) Sponsors

A quieter but equally powerful cousin of celebrity selling is cultivating **sponsors**. I don't mean commercial sponsors, like such-and-such a beer bringing you Monday Night Football on TV. I mean it as the word is used in select clubs and organizations — to get in, you need one or more **sponsors** to vouch for you and promote your membership. Sponsorships in business aren't always so formal, but they work the same way: Ben Tisinger, by introducing me into the society of Dallas shakers-and-movers was, in effect, my sponsor, in a club where my name, alone, would never have gotten me through the door.

Whether or not they've got a charter, by-laws and regular meetings, select groups of human beings are **clubs,** closed to outsiders, unless an influential insider wants you in. The more influence your insider has, the more influence you will have, as you become an insider.

When you're coming in under somebody's wing, pick the biggest, high-flying-est wing you can find!

The wing belongs to your sponsor, who will do two things for you, which you can't do on your own.

• She or he will bring you from **out**side to **in**side, and confer **influence** that might otherwise take you years to develop.

• Your sponsor will tell you and show you who's who and what's what, giving you immensely valuable information about personalities and inner workings of the group.

These two I-words, **influence** and **information**, always go together. They give each other enormous power.

Steve Anderson, our go-getter from Salt Lake City, is always doing more of what we all teach, with some pretty amazing results. Steve recently represented Planned Marketing Associates at a national convention of a certain professional association, whose members have been coming to our seminars in droves. The convention happened to be in the home city of the sponsoring association, and Steve arranged to tour the association's offices. He might know a dozen important members and officers who could have shown him around. But who took Steve around, making introductions? The association's president! Using NEER principles, with linkages of very influential contacts within the organization, it was perfectly comfortable, and appropriate, for this young guy to be squired around by the head honcho.

Were the folks who met Steve through the president more inclined to take note of him and what he had to say?

If you don't think this made any difference, you'd better go back to Page 1 and start reading again. If you still don't think so, by the time you get back here, one of us, the reader or the author, gets a big red **F** in NEER Marketing.

In one weekend, at that association meeting, Steve did a year's worth of business, meeting scores of highly interested prospects, and making many sales for our seminar program. I couldn't believe what I was hearing when he reported in on the phone! I told Steve he was getting more out of that meeting than I could have. This was not faint praise. At one time I did something like 80 percent of my insurance business at buyers' meetings and conventions. Working meetings is, indeed, a personal specialty, to which I devote a unit of the Planned Marketing seminars. Pretty soon you'll be able to read about these techniques, in the upcoming **How To Work A Meeting.** This is a booklet, rather than a book, so it'll be easier to carry in your pocket at meetings and conventions.

Of course, Steve would have acquitted himself well, whether or not the executive director took him around that association's home offices. He did better, though, because he went into the association's headquarters under such enormous, powerful wings.

Companies are another kind of club, where your selling power is greatly enhanced as you move from outsider to insider. Your **inside coach**, whom we introduced back in Chapter 7, **Close Encounters Of The NEER Kind**, acts as your sponsor, within the company club. (If you're fuzzy about who and what an inside coach is, you might want to go back and review the first part of that chapter.)

The inside coach works for a company to which you want to sell, but is not the person who buys. He or she steers you to the buyer, or buying team, and explains the personalities and inner workings of the company. The contact we described in Chapter 7 was pretty much a one-shot deal, to identify your selling targets and tactics. But the relationship, if it continues and deepens, can do much more for you. You can, by cultivating an inside coach, tap into a stream of inside information, learning what you would never know without the coach.

If your relationship with the inside coach is sufficiently trusting, and he or she is influential in the company, the coach functions exactly as a sponsor does in a select organization or group. He or she will introduce you around, and you'll benefit from the coach's influence and power.

5) Power Leads

In past chapters, we've already touched upon our next Door-Opener, developing and selling to **Power Leads**. In each market are buyers whose value to you far exceeds their individual sales potential. These are what my grocery-selling buddies and I used to call Bell Cows, the buyers that everybody else will follow. If you sell them, an enormous chunk of the market will, automatically, come along.

Here, as in all aspects of IQ, inside information is enormously important, so you can learn about the leadership and influence of certain buyers. Your **80/20** assessments of buyers, which is all about what they, themselves, are worth to you in potential sales, may not tell you anything at all about market leadership. All markets, large and small, have these power buyers, whose decisions are watched and imitated. They may not buy a lot, but they're worth all the time and effort you can give them. If they say Yes!, others will tell you the same thing.

All of these IQ Door-Openers are akin to **Celebrity Selling**, because they operate similarly: In each, you ally yourself and selling influence with a name better-known than yourself. **Celebrities** have the broadest, most generalized appeal. Anybody wants to meet you, when you can introduce them to somebody they can brag about meeting after they get home. **Event selling** often relies on the appearance of a celebrity. Even if there's nobody especially famous appearing, events are a species of showbiz, that draw people and put them into a festive mood. By **raising your own profile**, emceeing and public speaking, you increase your own celebrity, so people want to meet you, even when you're not standing next to a movie star or giving away balloons and door prizes.

Sponsors, the right kind of **Inside Coaches**, and **Power Leads** are, in effect, the celebrities of their organizations and circles of influence. People want to meet you because of them, and buyers are more inclined to say Yes! because of your association with them.

Think back to the chapters where we discussed N_1 and N_2 NEER relationships. The first category of IQ, Door-Openers, is related to N_1s. These are very high-powered ways of saying "Hello!" to buyers, so you'll get more attention and respect. Unlike basic N_1 relationships, which are one-on-one, these IQ Door-Openers are for meeting many buyers, so you're saying "Hello!" to entire markets.

X-ray Eyes: Looking For Value-Adders

One of the things that hasn't changed much, since I was a kid, are those mail-order catalogs for youngsters, with bird whistles, magnets, hot-air balloon kits, how-to books on hypnosis, magic tricks, and what-all. The mix of home science, magic and nasty jokes to play on your friends doesn't make much sense — unless you know the mind of a 12-year-old boy.

One of the hits, when I was a boy, were the X-ray glasses. I noticed not too long ago they're still selling them, with the same picture of a kid with his eyes bugged out because he's looking at somebody's skeleton. The glasses aren't nearly as good as the catalog copy. All you get is an optical illusion. You can't really see through anything.

NEER is about to give you, for free, without special lenses, what the kids' catalogs promised. You are about to develop **X-ray Vision!** Just like Superman, except you don't have to wear a funny outfit or be a nerd like Clark Kent.

NEER teaches you to look **through** your seller-buyer relationships, which turns out to be every bit as important as looking **at** them. Adding value is largely a matter of seeing beyond your sale and helping your buyer do more business with his or her buyers. In an established NEER relationship, your customer's customers become vitally important. If you want to sell big, you must sell **through**, all the way to your product's end-users.

I learned about sell-through very early in my career, when I represented Light Crust flour. The flour was really off our hands when the wholesalers bought it from Burrus Mills. Warehouse stock and the sacks of flour on store shelves were somebody else's property. But I couldn't treat that flour as somebody else's problem — not if I wanted to achieve conspicuous sales success.

No amount of salesmanship was going to get my buyers, the

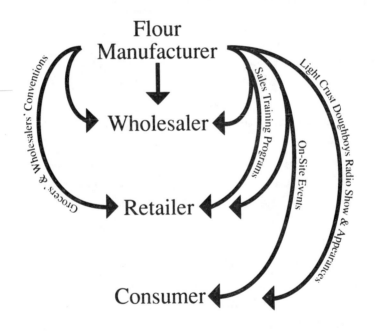

Sell through to the end user.
Add value EVERYWHERE!

wholesalers, to order more flour, unless I got their customers, the grocers, to order more flour. And the grocers weren't going to order more flour unless their customers, Ma And Pa Consumer, bought more.

When I worked Friday nights and Saturdays in supermarkets, playing country music, giving away door prizes and selling flour at special prices, I wasn't selling to my own customers — but my customers' customers' customers! I had to clear the grocery stores' shelves to clear the wholesalers' shelves, so they'd buy more boxcars and truckloads of flour.

Getting along well with your buyers is not enough. You must stimulate the buyers' growth. Not only will your volume go up, you'll cement the relationship with trust and loyalty, as the buyer learns to appreciate your contribution to his or her success, and relies increasingly on you. This is the power of the **Buyer For, Not Seller To** relationship.

• Think of whose shelves need to be cleared, and how you're going to do it.

• Always enhance your clients' relationships with their clients!

This enhancement can take many forms. You can sell through, or help the clients sell by sharing valuable information. I once scored a lot of points by training my clients' sales forces. Their companies liked me better and bought more, because they were selling more.

Back in Chapter 1, we talked about **Value**, which is anything and everything that makes your customers' purchases from you more worthwhile. In a sell-through situation, the key is to help them move more product. If your customers are end-users, you'll want to make sure they get the best possible use of your product or service, with training and on-site assistance. You can do well by offering assistance and training that is not directly related to your product, if such a program is needed. Virtually anything that makes you and what you represent more valuable can be considered. Add enough value, and you take the competition out of the game, because saying Yes! to you is the only sensible choice.

The simplest and most obvious component of value is **price**.

Reducing price can, in the short term, seem as good as adding value. I want to emphasize **seem**. Lower prices can get a first-time buyer, but price won't **keep** the buyer, if you don't start adding value. I put price at the bottom of my list of value-adders because I believe price is, ultimately, less important than stimulating clients' sales or helping them use your product better. These are the ingredients of the most long-term, productive, mutually profitable NEER relationships. Loyal, repeat customers are the real gold mine in selling. With repeat customers, more and more **buying** happens with less **selling** effort.

I've also put price after other value issues because the most important price cuts become possible only **after** you've established a Buyer For-Not Seller To relationship with a large client base. In your initial one-on-one relationships with buyers, the ability to cut price is narrowly limited by your suppliers' prices. When they run a sale or special promotion, you can pass along the savings. Beyond that, dealing down cuts into your own margin, which may not be big enough to cut.

All of this changes, though, as you move from selling to individuals to **selling to markets**. Large-volume selling gives you **economies of scale**. You can ask for preferential pricing from suppliers and get it, because of your importance in the market. As you gain volume and power you can create special products for your market. Custom-tailoring is as good as price reduction, because it gives clients more of what they want and need, and none of what they don't want. Generic products and services usually are an inefficient compromise for specialized users. A large part of the success of my own best NEER, selling insurance to grocers, was custom-tailoring policies and financial instruments, so buyers were getting just what they needed and wanted, and nothing else.

Finding the best ideas to add value to what you sell is a matter of developing your own powers of observation and understanding. The trick here is to stop focusing on your own business problems.

Study and help solve the problems of others. This is the quickest way to solve your own.

LQ: Your Leverage Quotient

Businessmen worry about Location the way folks down in the Caribbean worry about Voodoo. We've all known a storefront or a street-corner that is cursed by the Location Spirits. Business after business in these places goes from "Grand Opening" direct to "Liquidation Sale," about as quickly as the owners can change the signs. The cursed locations sit empty for a while, until somebody else signs the lease and tries another bright idea. Meanwhile, there are folks getting rich selling the same sort of stuff across the street, or down the block.

Location, alone, can't account for spectacular selling success. But it can play a very important role. Most really successful merchants and restaurateurs have set up shop in a place where there are a lot of people, who are the type of people who most want whatever is being sold. Lots of traffic, alone, does not mean success. You've got to have the right kind of traffic. This is why retailers and restaurants tend to cluster according to the socio-economic profiles of their clienteles.

But location is a matter of **time**, as well as **place**. You want to be **where** your clients are going to be **when** they are most likely to buy what you're selling.

Think about the Old Money types in your city. On a per-capita basis, these people are much more likely to own Mercedes cars, eat in little-bitty places with menus written in French, and buy season tickets to the opera. Does this mean you should put your new Mercedes showroom next to the Performing Arts Center? Of course not — people don't buy cars when they're going out for the evening. You might, however, do very well if you put an authentic French restaurant close to the opera house. You'd do better yet if you dreamt up a $6.50 chocolate fantasy dessert and called it **La Bohéme**.

Be **where** the right people are, **when** they're in a buying mood. This is the essence of location. Your **LQ — Leverage Quotient —** involves the same all-important where and when. LQ is location in the abstract, as it applies to NEER marketing systems. Once you've got a good idea, you must find the place to implement it so it has the greatest persuasive effect, on the greatest number of the most qualified buyers, at the moment they most want to buy.

In NEER systems we are only rarely talking about streets and street numbers. The principle is the same, though. When you're looking for leverage, it can help a great deal to visualize your target clients as shoppers, and their NEER systems as the malls and business districts where they circulate.

NEER systems work for all sellers for the same reason that well-established high-traffic business districts work for merchants. These systems are where the buyers are, when they feel like buying. Your challenge is to blend in with what's already in place, so buying from you is a natural, effortless extension of the business the buyers are already doing.

Lines of economic activity and influence converge at the best leverage-points. Whatever you do has the greatest effect, on the most people, without making them too aware of the effect you're having. In most cases, they'll buy more easily — and buy more — if they're less aware that you're selling. This is Stealth Sales, deadly effective when you penetrate deep into along standing NEER system.

For all our millions in receipts, my insurance company was just about invisible in our grower-to-grocer NEER system. The customers were more comfortable buying from us because we offered our services in a familiar, trusted system. Purchasing was much less resistable because we were an add-on to the monthly bills they were already paying. At least 80 percent of resistance is swept away when you enter an established, regular billing cycle. People don't fight

GROWERS

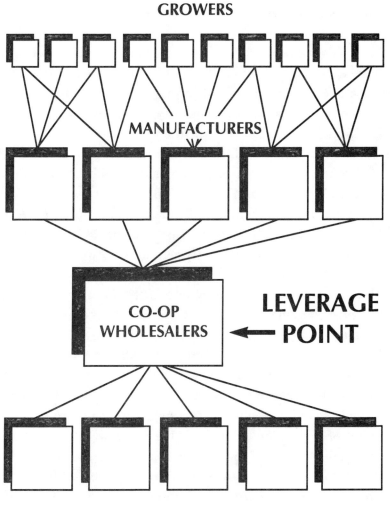

MANUFACTURERS

CO-OP WHOLESALERS ⟵ LEVERAGE POINT

INDEPENDENT GROCERS

know even you're there. Then, after you're too successful to ignore, you hold all the high ground, and they can't attack. My experience and observations show that once you have a few prominent members of a specialized market, the competition cuts and runs.

Payroll deduction is the ultimate established billing cycle. After a few weeks, the buyers totally forget they're buying. At that point, it takes a major decision to **quit** buying, which most people won't ever make. I once sold 80 percent of the employees of Morton's Potato Chip Co. in Dallas on an insurance and savings program just because the top honchos G.C. Morton and Van Ellis allowed me to offer the program through payroll deduction. All I had to do was set up a little table and let the people sign up on their breaks. The foreman brought them to the table and introduced us! A deal like this does away with at least 90 percent of resistance. Even if they didn't really like me or the program, they were much more likely to buy because of my inside position.

Always remember what the **N** in NEER stands for — Naturally Buying must come naturally to your clients. What comes most naturally is, most of the time, what they're already doing.

You may have a brand-new idea, which is the greatest thing since sliced bread, but you may not want it to **seem** as new as it is. This is how I worked my insurance marketing idea, which was so new people called it revolutionary. I made sure that, from the buyers' point of view, it looked and felt like business as usual. It all fit as **comfortably** as an old shoe.

People love to spend money, but they hate to be sold!

The most powerful mass distribution system for NEER marketing may be the **coop**, which is owned by its customers, usually small, independent businesses, to give them large-scale economic power. If you can convince a coop's management to offer your product or service, you have earned the prior approval of the buyers, because the coop is theirs, created for their mutual benefit and survival. When people bond for survival, as many people who form and join coops do, the sense of unity and trust is much stronger.

Individual businesses and professionals also band together in **associations** and other formal strategic alliances. These are not always, strictly speaking, NEERs, in that they don't generally involve buying and selling. They're more like near-NEERs. In principle, though, these organizations are the same as coops — individuals banding together for the common good, to push their political agendas at local, state and national levels, set standards for themselves, recognize outstanding achievement and share valuable information. They also confer the social and psychological benefits of solidarity. People who belong to a group are less lonely and vulnerable, and less afraid. If you can blend into buyers' groups and make valuable contributions, you become, from the buyer's point of view, **us**, instead of **them.** The difference, when you're selling, is enormous. Just ask our seminar alum who sells insurance, who worked his way into prominence in that medical professional association. He's now an officially endorsed supplier, which means those doctors are his officially endorsed customers!

Matching **ideas** and **leverage-points**, like everything else about selling, is as much art as science. What works with one product, and one clientele, at one particular leverage-point, may absolutely bomb with another.

When you're really fine-tuned and running on all your selling cylinders, you'll be using more than one idea at multiple leverage-points in your NEER systems. When I sold flour, I wasn't just playing records and handing out fresh-baked cookies in the supermarkets. I was also working every grocers' and grocery wholesalers' convention I could get to. And I trained the management and employees at my Bell Cow supermarkets, so they could sell better. Meanwhile, my company was sending the Light Crust Dough Boys all over the South, and the band was playing on the radio. A diagram of the whole business would look like acupuncture. Burrus

Mills and I had a needle stuck in every nerve-center, head to toe.

Try to use this principle of LQ all the time, whether or not you're looking for a place to implement your brightest business-building ideas. As we say here in the country, you always want to get two bites at the apple. Make sure you get the most out of every little bit of effort and time. You're never going to get any more. You cannot save these precious moments and opportunities.

ACTION PLAN

Pushing You Out Of The Nest

The Planning and the Action is now up to you.

This book is largely about **looking** for business. The goal is to make you a **CPA** — Creative Prospecting Activator. First we looked for the best prospects, then for the best ways to meet those prospects, through the best intermediary contacts. All this looking has been for **people.** You should now be looking beyond individuals to the **markets** they're part of. The idea is to discover ideas and leverage-points to multiply your selling, so you wield more and more influence with **groups** of buyers.

If you're awake, or even half-awake, you ought to be searching for this NEER selling power.

You'll know when you've got a great plan for using a great idea in a great place, because it will feel great. You'll know because you **know.** Even the most miserable, contrary and lazy reactive little guys in your head will shut up for a few glorious minutes, and start shouting **Eureka, I Have Found It!**

This feeling alone would justify the hunt for big ideas. But of course there are other rewards, once you get the right idea working for you, in the right place.

Between the big Eureka! and ultimate success lie hard work,

discouragement, probably some failures. Don't expect everything to work the first time, just because you know it's supposed to work. But don't forget that you **know** it's going to work. Keep trying. Try the same idea in a different place. Or, if you're in love with your leverage-point, make some idea adjustments.

I had to try NEER twice, and have it fail twice, before I found the most receptive bunch of people, in the perfect place, to take us all to heaven.

Never, ever forget that humankind's greatest accomplishments were made by people who were tired and discouraged and thinking about giving up.

Weariness and discouragement may be a sign that you're getting close to what you want.

Draw some diagrams. Flesh out a few brilliant ideas. Make some plans for putting IQ & LQ to work for you. Then do it!

12

OPEN: Other People's Experience Now!

RAISING YOUR IQ

Selling is at least 80 percent preparation. And preparation is at least 80 percent knowledge. Back in the early chapters of this book we tapped into a much-neglected source of knowledge that can do you more good in persuasive success than a university marketing degree. This knowledge is close-at-hand, and free. It is, actually, closer than your hand — it's between your own ears! The daily data-stream, from what you see and hear and do, is full of extremely valuable information about what you need to do — and need to stop doing — in order to be more successful. The trick is to recognize the value of that knowledge, and analyze it and, most important, use it.

You've got to know what you know!

The greater part of knowledge, though, is knowing what you don't know.

Those making real progress, in any walk of life, are increasingly aware of the limits of their own experience and knowledge. At the same time they feel an increasing hunger to share the wisdom of others. The ultimate source of information, and the whole world's living wisdom, lies in the minds of others.

An awful lot of pessimistic, deep-sounding philosophical nonsense has been written about how we human beings are isolated, and sharing experience is impossible, and we can't really learn from others. This is, as I just said, nonsense. You can learn what others know.

All you have to do is **ask!**

Somewhere, probably not too far from where you are right now, is somebody who knows whatever it is that you want to know. And he or she probably wants to share that knowledge. Chances are, though, that the knowledge has never been shared, because nobody has **asked!**

Whatever you're looking for is looking for you. And whoever you're looking for, is looking for you. I can't altogether explain this, but I know it's true, because I've witnessed the power of this principle in action, hundreds of times.

When the student is ready, the teacher appears!

The student isn't going to be ready, though, if he or she doesn't start asking.

We play a riddle game with our clients who come to seminars. We ask them this:

If there were a three-letter word that would guarantee you:

1) The key to beating the law of averages

2) Magic advice from mentors

3) Perceived equality with the most prestigious professionals

4) All the power and success of the top business persuaders, sales executives and attorneys

5) Tenfold increases in advertising results

6) Better marriage and family relationships

7) Increased personal income

8) Publicity

9) Savings on your purchases of up to 40 percent

10) Access to the genius of the Master Mind, more powerful than the greatest human thinkers

11) The Power of a Persuader with a Purpose

12) All the guidance and care that grandchildren get from their grandparents

If there were such a word, would you want to know it?

What do you think our clients say? Of course they want to know that word, right now!

The word, of course, is **ask.** It isn't magic, but it might as well be magic, for the wonderful power it confers, if you just use it.

Now I'm going to ask you a question:

If there were an intelligence you could tap into, greater than any living human being's, that could help you solve your most urgent business or personal problems, would you want to get in touch with it?

I'm hearing a big, loud Yes!

There is, indeed, such an intelligence. It is named in the 10th of the 12 good things that Ask can do for you.

Master Mind is what Napoleon Hill called the Infinite Intelligence that becomes accessible when two or more people meet in mutual understanding and harmony and shared purposes. Human intelligence, in the right combinations, multiplies. Two people who are deeply in-sync are smarter than the sum of their IQs. They can more than double their creative, constructive problem-solving ability, finding solutions that they'd never find on their own, in two lifetimes. Eight or ten people in a Master Mind group are so smart it's scary.

When like-minded individuals establish deep rapport and start thinking together, amazingly good ideas come to the fore. And good things start to happen for everybody involved. The results exceed expectations every time. I know this works, because I've seen it work. But I can't altogether explain it. Spiritual types see spiritual forces at work. Those who are religious see the hand of God in the Master Mind principle. Even the most dyed-in-the-wool doubters and atheists admit that there is extraordinary creative power in a gathering of like-minded individuals. Groups can solve problems beyond the grasp of any individual. People in groups are, in a word, smarter.

I know I didn't start to get really smart, in business, until I formed my own Master Mind group, after I got the idea from Napoleon Hill's *Think And Grow Rich,* the business motivational classic that changed my life. Some friends of mine, who also had their own businesses and big ambitions, came over to my house at the crack of dawn. We did calisthenics, listening to motivation records (this was before tape cassettes). Then we brainstormed, offering ideas and suggestions to help solve each other's business and personal problems. Absolutely any pressing need, for which others could offer ideas and support, was our subject-matter.

To this day I bring important problems to a Master Mind group, made up of very successful business people from all over. Some members fly to the meetings. Everyone gives up extremely high-priced working time. But an hour or two with the Master Mind is worth it. Each of us, working in that group, is smarter than we could hope to be, all by ourselves.

To find your ultimate business successes, you must also get smarter than you are now, and smarter than you could ever hope to be, all by yourself. You must learn more and never stop learning. Now is the time to link up with others.

• **Ask** for the information you need. Develop relationships with

mentors. If they've gone where you want to go, they know what you need to know.

• Form a **Master Mind** mental and spiritual alliance, with like-minded individuals who share your values and goals. If you're going to the same place, group travel is the way to go.

Learning From the Experienced

Sometimes the sayings the old folks taught us, which were supposed to be wisdom, were just plain wrong. "What you don't know can't hurt you," is about as wrong as you can get.

Sometimes, though, the sayings were merely misspelled. Case in point is that old saw, "Experience is the best teacher." Somebody along the line dropped a letter and changed the grammar. The real wisdom is this:

The experienced are the best teachers!

Experience isn't such a bad teacher, if you've got a lot of time and money. But if you want to know how to do something — without waiting for four or five years of trial-and-error to teach you — find somebody who has done what you want to do. When you find her or him, ask "How did you do it?" Chances are she'll tell you. Chances are, indeed, that she has been waiting a long time for you to show up and ask.

I don't know where the need is greater — among those who need the knowledge and counsel of **mentors,** or among mentors, who need somebody to teach and advise. We'll let the thinkers work on this. What's important is that you, the **doer,** require the assistance of mentors so you can accomplish more. Somewhere, not far from where you are now, is somebody who has solved the problems you're now working on. You probably know who that person is, but have been reluctant to approach and ask for advice.

The same things that keep you from calling your ideal buyers—all of that **False Evidence Appearing Real** — can keep you from making other kinds of much-needed contacts. We human beings are strange, contrary creatures. If you hold somebody in very high esteem, it's very easy to let **respect** and **admiration** become obstacles to meeting that person. The silent assumption is that somebody so successful wouldn't want to meet you. This is absolutely, 180 degrees wrong.

Respect and **admiration** are reasons, maybe the **only** reasons, to meet someone. You should use such feelings as a compass, to point you toward people. As for being an object of respect and admiration — as the mentors you want to meet are — your feelings of high regard are, really and truly, reasons why your mentors want to meet you. It feels great to be admired, and to spend time with someone who is truly interested in you and what you know. It feels good to be a mentor!

A while back we talked about CR — Call Reluctance — which stands between sellers and buyers. Remember how we took care of CR?

• First came **self-esteem** work. If you want others to **B**elieve in and **L**ike and **T**rust you, you've got to have BLT with yourself.

• Then came **NEER**, the system of making contacts through intermediary contacts, so you'll always be received with attention and respect.

If you're suffering from **MR** — Mentor Reluctance — and are afraid to approach the people you most admire, to ask for advice, the remedies are very similar.

• You've got to know that you are worth a great person's time and attention. You are, whoever you are. The Good Lord didn't decide to make junk the day you were born. You must know, too, that your interest in your mentor and his or her valuable experience is sincere and constructive.

• The NEER techniques, building bridges of influential intermediary contacts, will take you to whoever you need to meet. You're closer to meeting your heroes than you think. And your mentors-to-be **want** you to have that access.

Aim high, when you're searching for mentors. High is where you should always aim, in interpersonal contacts, in goal-setting, in everything.

Tips for finding ideal mentors:

• Look for **results**. They should be the closest possible match to what you want to do. A mentor's achievements should be recognized and respected, and he or she should be known for high integrity.

• There will be **understanding** of your problems, and you'll speak the same language. Most likely your mentor will be in the same field, or a very closely related one. If you own a fried chicken chain and aspire to make a million dollars, don't ask a millionaire knee surgeon how he made his.

• Your mentor will be ready to **share**. His or her success will be established and recognized. Older individuals are often the best mentors, because they've run their races and won and no longer feel competitive with you.

• You share **values**, of all kinds. Mentoring becomes a personal process, and the more you are spiritually in-sync, in agreement on big and small issues, the deeper the exchange can be.

In mechanics, meeting your ideal mentor is not all that different from any other NEER-style contact. You target someone and, using a chain of referrals, arrive with the warm recommendation of someone the mentor respects. When you call to make an appointment, ask for 7 minutes, at his or her convenience. Any longer, on the first visit, is an imposition, unless you're asked to stay longer. Arrive on time. Once introductions are over, tell the mentor what you know about his or her accomplishments, which should be quite a bit. And say why his or her knowledge and experience seems valuable to you. Then **ask** if the mentor would be willing to share a bit of that knowledge and experience.

If I had to bet, I'd wager on a Yes! no matter who you are, and whom you're approaching. Chances are this sincere request will be answered in the affirmative. I have never had a prospective mentor tell me no. And I have asked scores of recognized experts for advice.

Savor the moment, when your mentor says Yes! You have begun one of the most rewarding relationships in life. Many cultures recognize the mentor-pupil relationship as holy. Never forget to give this relationship the profound respect that you owe it.

Once you find a mentor, you must perfect the art of being mentored. Unless you do your part, sincerely and whole-heartedly, the relationship cannot flower, and both of you may come away with negative feelings.

• Respect the mentor's time. At the outset of each meeting, tell how much time you'll need. Take no more, unless it is offered.

• Be straight-forward. A hidden agenda of any kind will spoil everything. Don't try to sell a mentor anything or otherwise try to initiate a business relationship. The mentor may, eventually, want to bring business into the relationship. But the initiative is never yours.

• Keep your ears open and your mouth closed unless you're asking a thought-through question, or telling your mentor that you hear and understand.

• Pay your mentor back, and then some. Not in money, but invisible, audible **gratitude.** Say thanks for the information when you get it, and say thanks again, later. Keep in touch and give progress reports. The mentor wants to know what you're doing with the information and advice he or she gave. Third party appreciation is particularly gratifying. Let your mentor hear from others how thankful you are.

• As you progress, you'll need new mentors, for new challenges. You'll outgrow some of the mentors who helped you make progress, and your contacts with them will be become less frequent. But don't lose touch entirely. Inevitably, sooner or later, your old mentors will need some help from you. Give it freely.

This book begins and ends at the same place — mentors. I dedicated it to my mentors, too numerous to name on the dedication page. If those people hadn't taken an interest, and shared what they knew, I wouldn't be sharing what I know with you now. Without those mentors, I probably wouldn't have a whole lot worth sharing!

The Biggest Brain of All

The combined power of tapping into the wisdom and experience of others is, in our NEER System equation, an acronym. M^3. This stands for the mighty intelligence-raising potentialities of **Me**ntors and the **M**aster **M**ind. Get these three Ms working for you and you're a genius, even if you currently have trouble remembering how to tie your shoes. If you're already a genius, with a MENSA membership to prove it, you still need M^3 to achieve super-human intelligence, to discover and implement the ideas for super business success.

The three Ms came to me all at once, after that horrible night when the pig farmer burned down my ego, and I decided to go into a field that wouldn't do the kind of damage that selling insurance had just done to me. I didn't know the word yet, but it was a **Mentor** who turned me around. I told my troubles to my friend Ed Holman, my business "coach." He was a great coach that day — he sent me right back into the game, telling me I couldn't get out, because I'd never really been in. I owe him a lot for that one.

Coach Holman did more than send me back in, though. He gave me a new playbook, Napoleon Hill's *Think And Grow Rich,* which changed my life. The part of that classic that excited me most was the chapter on the Master Mind principle. I set the book down and started recruiting local businessmen I knew and respected for early morning workouts and skull sessions at my house. Out of that Master Mind group came the idea that made me rich.

It came up pretty much by accident. One of the fellows said I ought to call on the Affiliated Grocers Warehouse in Dallas, to sell them insurance. To tell the truth, this guy was not one of my favorites in the group. But the idea sounded reasonable, so I decided to call on Affiliated.

Please note that this was a little idea — selling some insurance **to** Affiliated — which was not the Big Idea — selling **through** Affiliated. But if that guy hadn't given me the little idea, I would not have had the big one. And if I hadn't been exercising my mental idea muscles, working out with my Master Mind group, I would not have been ready for a big idea. If I had it, I might not have known what to do with it.

A Master Mind generates valuable ideas spontaneously. They just start floating up. And it makes you much more open to ideas. The influence of the Master Mind makes you more ready to apply those new ideas, and bolder in the scale in which you're willing to try them. The ideas just flow, bigger and better, and bigger and better things start to happen.

Our clients sometimes have a hard time distinguishing between PARTNEER and Master Mind groups. They are, indeed, similar, in that they involve forming groups of individuals with good rapport and trust, who help each other advance. But they operate on entirely different levels. PARTNEER's focus is narrow, and entirely economic. You help each other find leads, period. The only business at hand is to increase each other's sales.

If PARTNEER is Trade School, Master Mind is a personal PhD program. The entire universe of ideas is open to a Master Mind. All areas of life are open, and none closed, to your allies, as long as the exchange is constructive, life-promoting and confidential. Exchanges must be entirely open within the Master Mind, but hermetically sealed from outsiders.

The alliance works to help members improve and actualize

themselves in all dimensions. Among business people the focus will, naturally, be on business, but allies might be asked for input on family or personal problems.

The guidelines and techniques for forming a PARTNEER group, spelled out in Chapter 9, are useful in forming a Master Mind. Remember, though, that the group's subject-matter is much broader, and the necessary levels of trust and rapport deeper. You are, in effect, appointing your cosmic board of directors. Since the purpose is not narrowly economic, membership is open to virtually anybody, so long as that person is a high-achiever, with high integrity, worthy of your respect and trust. The more fascinating the mix, the more fascinating the synergies and input. Remember this, though: One rotten apple in the bunch, and you'll have more of a Messed-Up Mind, than a Master Mind.

Meetings follow roughly the same format as those in PARTNEERships, with each member taking the floor for an allotted, brief period. He or she should give a capsule version of recent progress and then tell about a problem of pressing interest. The others then chime in with insights and suggestions, according to individual expertises and unique points-of-view. A Master Mind group, when it really gets cooking, is one of the greatest intellectual and emotional thrills imaginable. It seems almost sinful, that something so mutually profitable should be so much fun. The harder you work at it, the more fun it is.

Since the rapport is deeper, and more delicate, and the interchanges more intense, the size of Master Mind groups is limited. A dozen seems to be the magic number, for reaching the maximal critical mass. Groups of under five can be low on wattage. More than 12, and synergies start to cool off.

ACTION PLAN

Marching Orders

You have, once again, your marching orders. The instructions you need are in this chapter.

- Make a list of the ten people whose experience and knowledge would be most helpful to your business problems.
- Pick the person listed above you need to meet most. Using NEER techniques to prepare the way, make contact and establish and nurture a mentor relationship.
- Ask!
- Cultivate a second mentor.
- ASK!
- Keep cultivating, until you've got the Mentors you need.
- **ASK!**
- Form a Master Mind Alliance, with meetings at least every other week. Ask for, and give, the best insight and support and ideas.

ASK!

Charlie Revisited

Selling, when you go at it wrong, can be the least rewarding, most humiliating way to make a living in the world.

But, with an education in the Art And Science Of Persuasion, it is the most high-paying, interesting, life-affirming vocation of all.

The education never stops. One reading of this book, if you work to understand and **use** NEER, ought to bring some pretty startling successes. Don't stop there, though. Re-read, and you'll find new insights and NEER techniques and ideas to put to work for you. Keep studying NEER, and you'll keep surprising yourself. The system grows and advances with you. We just had an attorney who was Phi Beta Kappa at his law school come through our three-day seminar for the third time. Every time, he says, advanced his understanding of NEER and how he can use it. And he's not done with us yet!

Keep your mind and your eyes open, and you'll never be done with NEER. And it will never be done with you.

Back at the beginning of this book, we introduced a man we called Charlie, who began a new career selling insurance last year. He was full of promise and eagerness, but immediately ran into a wall of disappointment and failure. Charlie had all the looks and intelligence and likability for success in persuasion, but failed because he didn't have the **markets** he needed. Raw ability, without ready access to qualified buyers, got him absolutely nowhere. At the outset of what should have been a great career, he was going broke and suffering terribly.

The very first time we met Charlie — before he went into insurance sales — he was wearing a big, bright **9** on his forehead. Just after the insurance company loosed Charlie onto the world, with all sorts of in-house "training" but absolutely no nuts-and-bolts **preparation** for the real world, his self-esteem number was down to **4**, and sinking rapidly. Just listening to him on the phone was a lesson in agony. We could see he was in trouble from 20 yards away.

I got another look at Charlie recently. Once again we were giving a seminar on career change and finding new employment, in the city where we met him last year. I glanced over the podium and there he was, looking every bit as good as he had the first time we met him, before that insurance company's management set him up for a long, hard fall. No, he really looked **better** than he did when met him. His forehead number was 9.5 this time, if not higher. With a dozen rows of people between Charlie and me, I could see that something terrific had happened to him, and that he had come to see us to share exactly what it was. I was, naturally, dying to know. At the first break in the seminar, my associates — who had also seen him and noticed the change — and I visited with him.

Charlie told us his story:

After the last meeting with us, when he'd been in the insurance business for 30 days, he made a commitment to himself similar to the one that I made when I got really serious about the insurance business: He was not going to **get out** of the business until he **got in**.

It became clear, though, that he was not getting the kind of market-building support he wanted, and needed. It was painfully obvious that the management of the company he had chosen was not prepared, nor would it ever be prepared, to help a new agent build a business. He also came to the conclusion that he didn't need to blame himself for his discouraging start. Only one person in the class of 10, with whom Charlie was hired and trained, had stayed with the company! Many got out of sales altogether.

These were the kind of results a mediocre **Re-Active Manager(RAM)** had achieved at one of the most well-known life insurance companies in America. If that manager is not in trouble today for those results, it is only a matter of time before his company is in deep, deep trouble.

Charlie didn't want to quit — he wanted to **change**. So he started studying other major insurers, looking for a company in-sync with his values and goals. He wanted an employer that would give him help and support cultivating **markets**, that recognized the importance of being **out** with buyers, rather than **in** the office.

Charlie sought, and before long he **found**. The company he liked had more humble offices, and less impressive presentation materials, but it put its money and resources where they counted — developing markets. When he saw what he wanted, Charlie made a move.

The combination of company support and **NEER** principles of persuasion have brought Charlie more success than he's ever known. He's making a nice living, becoming a leading producer, and enjoying what he's doing immensely. Has Charlie made it? No, not yet. He's got some huge plans for himself. After our last visit I'm very confident he'll reach his goals, whatever they are.

Such success stories are the ultimate reward for me and the Planned Marketing Associates team. I wish we could take all of the credit, but sometimes I feel that we are just bystanders. The real heroes are the NEER system and people like you, who show a wonderful willingness to **learn** and **change**. I congratulate you for your persistence and for your enthusiasm to take the next step, putting into action a system that has the power to dramatically improve your persuasive success. I wrote this book to make NEER accessible to everyone. This system changed my life. It has helped many people enjoy Charlie's kind of victory. Now it is your turn to achieve the personal victory that lies in your future when you use the practical persuasive principles of the NEER system.

A partial list of mentors who have helped in so many areas of my life:

Mother
Dad
2 Grandfathers
2 Grandmothers
Kirby Albright
Al Altwegg
Dub and
   Mary Lou Anderson
Steve Anderson
Carlos Angelo
Louis Arrigoni
Doug Ash
Jud Ashmore
Ben Barnes
Greg Barnes
Nancy Barnes
Sam Beard
Bill Beaty
Brad Benbow
Jack Bertoglio
Gerald Bolfing
Jim and Jimmie Boyd
Taylor Boyd
Bill Bradfield
Gaylord Briley
L. D. Brinkman
Rene Brooks
Tom Brower
Lillian Bushnell
Tim Calabrese

Roger Cameron
Canadian Dental Association
Curt Carlson
Byron Carter
Pat Cashman
Barbara Cashwell
Cliff Cassidy
Jack Chandler
George Chapman
Chiropractors
Roger Chapman
Gordon Christensen
Devane Clark
Harold Clark
Jim Clayton
Doug and Beverly Coats
J. W. Colvin
John and Nellie Connally
Jack Conreaux
Ken Cooper
Francisco Coronado
Bill Cothrum
John Dalton
Jimmie Daniel
Pete and Jodie Dawson
Vern and
   Barbara Dockendorf
Peggy Dunbar
Glen DuPont
Gipp DuPree

Louise Edwards
Ted Edwards
Van and Lou Ellis
Ted Eubank
Jack Evans
Buckner Fanning
Billie Farrar
Ben Fauber and
    K-Mart Staff
Ed Foreman
Jno Freeman
Tom and Cindy Friedberg
Ralls Fulgham
Chuck Gaines
Harold Garbers
Bert Gerding
Garland Gibbs
Nat and Blanche Gibbs
Tracy and Kay Gilbreth
Alice Ginot
E. B. Gober
Barbara Graul
Ace Greenberg
Herb Greenberg
Grocery sales people selling
    Light Crust Flour
Larry Grove
Earl Gunn
Bob Haden
Burt, Anne, Jack and
    Mike Hailey
Sue Hailey
Morris and Nez Hall

Tom Harbison
Ray Hard
Lavern and Faye Harris
Inos Heard
Harland Helzer
    Other Co-op
    Warehouse Managers
John and Madelyn Hicks
Steve Hicks
Tom Hicks
Walter Hill
Ed Holman
J. R. Holt
Frank and
    Mary Grace Horlock
Megan Horton
C. C. Huffhines
Stuart and Jean Hunt
Sherman and Mary Hunt
Royce Hunter
Elaine Hurt
Bob Hutchins
Joleen Jackson
Michel Jahjah
Bert Jaqua
Jesus
Kerry Johnson
Kevin Johnson
George Jordan
Erla Kay
David and Marge Keener
Bill Kennedy
Jim Kenney

Art Kinsman
Carl Kruger
Loncy and Betty Leak
Mac and Carol Ann Lee
Mickey Lemaistre
Robert Lindberg
George Little
Jimmie Joe Lung
John Mahaffey
Imtiaz Manji
Mariano and
  Wanda Martinez
Maxie Maultsby
Jack Mazier
Joan and John McCollom
Sonny and Billie McCutchin
George McDonald
Tom McDougal
Travis McFee
David McMahon
Jo McSherry
Dude Meenach
Doug Miller
Wally Minto
Roger Mize
Marve and
  Kathleen Montgomery
Raymond Moreland
Ralph Moten
John and Lupe Murchison
Jack and Judy Murphy
Ted Newton
Anthony Nicholas

Woody Oakes
Marjan Oakeson
Orthodontists
George Owens
Luther and
  Mary Ann Parker
Largent Parks
Scranton Peevy
Periodontists
Banker Phares
Gil and Mary Phares
Bum and Debbie Phillips
Bob Polkgladnik
Randy Price
Jimmy Pritchett
Les Pritchett
Si and Kathy Ragsdale
Ranger Insurance Company
Jay Rodney Reece
Gene and Julia Reilly
Ralph Reilly
Willard Rhodes
Herb Ripply
Pete Roach
Parkes Robinson
Walter Robinson
Mike and
  Sharon Robinowitz
Ike Rolader
Milt Rosenzweig
Darrell and Edith Royal
Sam Rubin
John Russell

Ralph Sanders (FFA)
Ken Schmidt
Bill and Joan Schreyer
G. C. Schutts
Lewis Schutts
Scout Master (Mr. Pharr)
  and others helping me
  become Eagle Scout
Edgar Seaton
Darlene Sewell
Gene and Sara Shands
Bud Shaner
Legerwood Sloan
Bill and Peggy Smith
William G. Smith
Gerald Sormrude
Doc and Liz Spain
W. I. Sparks
Staff
Ken Staggs
Perky Staggs
Jim and Donna Stalker
Mike Steere
Bobby Stewart
Johnny Stewart
Bill Strange
Tommy and
  Shirley Strausburger
Bob Strauss
Larry Stutsman
Jim and Bunny Sullivan
Teachers (Virginia Steele)
Wally Tenega

Lou Tice
Ben and Millie Tisinger
Joe Tuck
Barney Vanston
Ed Vanston
Henry Wade
Tommy Walker
  and Goldman Sachs Group
Mary Walters
Roland Walters
Ade and Annabelle Ward
Taylor Wharton
Chuck White and
  Sigma Phi Epsilon
  Fraternity
Donna White
Jim Whited
Philip Whittlsey
Carl Wigglesworth
Dewitt Wilkerson
Bud Wilkinson
Art Wilson
Larry Wilson
Robert Witt
Angus Wynne
Zig Ziglar

Y.P.O. and World Business
   Council Board & Members
   whom I've been with for 35 years

Thousands of my fellow men so willingly
   gave me answers and help when I had
   sense enough to ask

Thank you

And the thousands who have so generously
   and patiently listened to thousands of
   speeches, sales meetings, and Power of
   Persuasion seminars and boot camps

If YES! Means SUCCESS In Your Business, You Need NEER!

WALTER HAILEY AND PLANNED MARKETING ASSOCIATES

After spectacular successes in business, self-made insurance magnate Walter B. Hailey began sharing his **N**aturally **E**xisting **E**conomic **R**elationship marketing system. Mr. Hailey embarked on his new career as a teacher and trainer in 1987. Almost immediately, his 3-day **NEER** seminars at Hailey's Canyon Springs Ranch in the Texas Hill Country were booked up months in advance, and companies clamored for on-site training. Mr. Hailey and his Planned Marketing Associates team now conduct seminars at the ranch and on the road, and give tailored training, consultations and speeches. Clients range from multibillion-dollar giants such as AT&T to family businesses and one-person sole proprietorships. Whatever the scale of the operations, all have benefitted from Mr. Hailey's straightforward lessons about how to create an ever-growing stream of more qualified, less resistant buyers. Those who master the **NEER** System never call cold, and never deal with strangers.

Although **NEER** has been principally taught to sellers, the system works for anybody who needs to hear "Yes!" to make students get higher grades, charities increase their contributions, and doctors build rapport with their patients. Virtually anybody can get more out of business, and out of life, with **NEER**. To remind us of the universal applicability of **NEER**, Mr. Hailey addresses his system to **Persuaders**, rather than just to those directly involved in sales and marketing. A Persuader is someone who must hear "Yes!" to succeed. By this definition, we are all Persuaders.

So confident is Mr. Hailey in his system that his training includes a money-back guarantee. If **NEER** doesn't boost productive results at least 20 percent, however results are measured, Planned Marketing Associates will make a full refund of fees. Mr. Hailey and his team are constantly adding to Planned Marketing's catalog of quality products, which now includes audio and video tapes, books and booklets. These materials, like **NEER** itself, are designed to help people hear "Yes!" more often, more easily, from those whose "Yes!" means most. The lessons Planned Marketing teaches will get you through the doors you need to get through, with all the prestige and influence you need.

Call or write Planned Marketing today, to find out how America's most dynamic professional development company can help you in **Breaking The NO Barrier!**

Planned Marketing Associates
P.O. Box 345
Hunt, TX 78024
Phone (210)238-4357
Toll Free (800)460-0275
FAX (210)238-4075

We thank you for reading this book, and would appreciate any comments or criticisms. Call, and we're all ears. Write, and we'll read every word and write back.

Prices for additional copies of **Breaking The NO Barrier**:
1-5 copies $19.95 each
6-15 copies $14.95 each
more than 15 copies $9.95 each

Include $3.50 shipping and handling for every two copies. Order more than 15, and we pay shipping and handling. Texas residents pay 6.75 percent sales tax.

Break All Your No Barriers With The Yes System!

BREAKING
THE
NO
BARRIER

The Billion Dollar Battle Plan for getting everyone you want
to say YES to your proposition.

By Walter Hailey

The "run away seller" that reveals the revolutionary selling and persuasion system that Walter Hailey has used with thousands of professionals, entrepreneurs, and sales people across America to build their businesses and their careers. Hailey used this system to generate over $1 billion dollars of business in less than eight years. These same tested principles will help you to multiply your personal and professional results immediately.

YES! I want to order_____ copy(s) of **BREAKING THE NO BARRIER**

1-5 copies $15.95 per copy.

6-12 copies $13.95 per copy.

13+ copies $11.95 per copy.

Please add $3.50 minimum shipping and handling. $3.50 shipping and handling for every two copies. We pay the shipping for orders over 12 copies!

(Texas residents are required to pay 6.75% sales tax.)

NAME: _____

COMPANY: _____

MAILING ADDRESS:_____

CITY:_____STATE:_____ZIP: _____

PHONE:(____) _____

CIRCLE ONE: VISA   MC   AMEX   CARD#_____EX: ___/__

OR CHECK ENCLOSED FOR $ _____

TO ORDER:

MAIL THIS FORM TO PLANNED MARKETING P.O. BOX 345 HUNT, TEXAS 78024

OR

FAX THIS ORDER FORM TO (210) 238-4075

OR

PHONE ORDERS ARE TAKEN AT 1-800-HUNT-TEXAS (1-800-486-8839).

PLANNED MARKETING ASSOCIATES, INC. P.O. BOX 345 HUNT, TEXAS 78024 (210) 238-4357.